Historical Walks

The Gatineau Park Story

Third Edition

Katharine Fletcher

Maps by Eric Fletcher

Fitzhenry & Whiteside

Historical Walks: Third Edition
Copyright © 2004 Katharine Fletcher

In Canada:
    Fitzhenry & Whiteside Limited, 195 Allstate Parkway, Markham, Ontario L3R 4T8
In the United States:
    121 Harvard Avenue, Suite 2, Allston, Massachusetts 02134
    www.fitzhenry.ca godwit@fitzhenry.ca

Fitzhenry & Whiteside acknowledges with thanks the Canada Council for the Arts, the Government of Canada through its Book Publishing Industry Development Program, and the Ontario Arts Council for their support of our publishing program.

10 9 8 7 6 5 4 3 2 1

National Library of Canada Cataloguing-in-Publication

Fletcher, Katharine, 1952-
    Historical walks : the Gatineau Park story / Katharine Fletcher ; maps by Eric Fletcher.

Includes index.
ISBN 1-55041-772-X

1. Gatineau Park (Quebec)--History. 2. Hiking--Quebec (Province)--
Gatineau Park--Guidebooks. 3. Trails--Quebec (Province)--Gatineau Park--Guidebooks. 4.
Gatineau Park (Quebec)--Guidebooks. I. Fletcher, Eric, 1951- .II. Title.

FC2799.P3F44 2004   971.4'221   C2003-900907-6
F1054.G26F44 2004

US Cataloging-in-Publication Data
(Library of Congress Standards)

Fletcher, Katharine, 1952-
Historical walks : the Gatineau Park story / Katharine Fletcher ; maps by Eric Fletcher. –3rd ed.
[p.208] : ill. , maps ; cm.
Includes bibliographical references.
Summary: A history, guidebook and travel reference to Gatineau Park, Ottawa, Canada.
ISBN 1-55041-772-X (pbk.)
1. Gatineau Park (Québec) -- History. 2. Hiking -- Quebec (Province) -- Gatineau Park --
Guidebooks. 3. Trails -- Quebec (Province) -- Gatineau Park -- Guidebooks. I. Title.
971.4/221 21   F1054.G25F44 2004

Cover / Interior design by Karen Petherick

All maps were designed by Eric Fletcher
Printed and bound in Canada

This book is dedicated to my mother who taught me never to say "can't," and who instilled within me an unceasing curiosity for, and love of, our precious natural world.

Contents

Preface

Since I first self-published *Historical Walks* in 1988 (and its second edition in 1998), I have sold over 11,000 copies. It's a well-established Canadian regional bestseller. I'm delighted that its third edition is in capable hands, and trust that my book will continue to introduce park visitors to the human and natural history of this precious sanctuary only twenty minutes north of Ottawa.

The National Capital Commission (NCC) — the Crown agency mandated with managing the park — continues to be confronted with challenges from park users. And of course there have been many changes to Gatineau Park since my first edition in 1988. Now in-line and ski-skaters join bicyclists on the Parkway system, enjoying the paved roads that wend through spectacular woodland scenery. Today, equestrians can ride along the western sector of Gatineau Park, starting from a stable based at Luskville Falls in the municipality of Pontiac (see Luskville Falls walk).

Other changes are not so positive for those of us who have known Gatineau Park over the course of thirty years or more. Vanished are the delightful old wooden signs naming trails like "Petticoat Lane," or "George's Trail." These signposts to history were replaced by an efficient but sterile numbering system devoid of insight into the rich human history of the park's network of trails. *Historical Walks* provides the only extant record of these old names. And heritage buildings within the park, such as the Capucin Chapel on Meech Lake perhaps exist only on a wish and a prayer. Once the Capucin friars welcomed a hundred or so Meech Lake cottagers to their inter-denominational services on many a summer Sunday. Today perhaps one or two paddle over to pray here, and the Capucin brothers are growing old. What will become of this beautiful park institution? Can it survive?

Users continually place demands upon the park which directly impact wildlife as well as the sanctuary and peace enjoyed by other visitors. In the recent past, mountain bikers in particular have disregarded the shared trail network, biking on any trail they choose regardless of its designation. Gatineau Park Director Jean René Doyon told me that constant public dialogue between the NCC and groups such as bikers is beginning to pay off. Notably, Doyon said, bikers are realizing that not all trails are appropriate for their activity. He notes, "We are seeing a change in the level of our discussions. People realize they don't have a right to access everything in the park. There has to be compromise. The solution, really, is limiting access. We need to think of what we value in a park, and discuss it freely so we can come to some agreement."

Overall, however, I think Gatineau Park serves its more than one million annual visitors well. Since 2000, its trails link to the rest of Canada via the Trans-Canada Trail, the longest recreational corridor in the world. The Trans-Canada Trail follows segments of several trails, such as the Discovery Trail (#36) along Meech Lake, so we can hike, ski, and bike along a pathway that is truly part of the warp and weft of Canada.

Historical Walks proudly recalls the human history of what many Ottawa residents consider "the jewel in the crown" of the National Capital Region's greenspace. This edition offers updated information, updated maps, and new snippets of history. I hope you enjoy learning the park's secrets while hiking, biking, horseback riding, skiing, in-line skating, snowshoeing, or otherwise exploring its network of trails.

Katharine Fletcher
Quyon, Quebec
January 2004

Special Notes to My Readers: For readability, bibliographic references have been gathered as Endnotes in the final pages. I have used the following abbreviations in the text: some photographs bear the acronym "NAC" for the National Archives of Canada; and "n.d." means "not dated." Similarly, "NCC" is National Capital Commission; "FDC" is Federal District Commission; and "HSG" refers to Historical Society of Gatineau. It should be noted, too, that as of January 2003 this organization has altered its name to Gatineau Valley Historical Society.

Preface to the second edition

In the first edition of *Historical Walks*, published in August 1988, I wrote that the book was the culmination of three years work. Today, as I present you with the second edition, complete with new and updated trails, photos and history, another nine years has passed ... I realize how much more I've learned about Gatineau Park, its human and natural history, and its paths, lookouts, and tantalizing ruins of homesteads. Even so, as I send this manuscript to the printer, I realize there's so much more to write. Every year that passes introduces me to readers and keen hikers, skiers, canoeists, and bikers who have stories to share, who know of "hidden treasures" like a meadow of lupins or who have an old photo to show. As such stories emerge, as new trails are made (and old ones rerouted), I know there's a continued demand for new editions of this book. This gives me great pleasure. Why? Because for me Gatineau Park is a lifelong love whose secrets continue to unfold with each passing season.

Your interest in my book reflects, I believe, a shared desire to connect with nature. In our helter-skelter world, I believe Gatineau Park offers us the repose and restorative effects of sanctuary. Our park is not only a wildlife reserve where plants such as the wild leek and creatures such as the white-tailed deer are protected. No, Gatineau Park is a sanctuary that nurtures the soul.

It is here within the park that we experience and connect with the cleansing renewal of the seasons. May is the month of joyous birth, with the drama of rushing waterfalls and the wondrous carpet of trillium, spring beauty, and hepatica swaying in the warm breezes that stir the forest floor. Then there is July's heavy humidity, when the fawn hugs the side of the doe in the thicket, when the cicadas' drone splits summer's heavy heat asunder. The flamboyant artist named October paints leaves with brilliance, closely followed by early November's dark promise of rain and sleet. Then snowfall's quiet descends. This is the time of the storytelling, when park lodges rock to the laughter of skiers, spinning tall tales of daring around the old wood stoves ...

Since first conceiving *Historical Walks* in 1985, I have come to recognize the inevitability of change. In today's park, sightseers crowd the parkways in autumn, enjoying the colours in the predominantly hardwood forests. But the woods were not always so. In the Depression of the 1930s jobbers cleared woodlots for a dollar or two, creating a patchwork quilt effect in the landscape just to the north of Canada's capital. It was public pressure that created Gatineau Park, along with the political will of Prime Ministers King and Bennett, and the vision of planner Jacques Gréber. More change came to pass in 1994, when once-expropriated sections of the Meech Creek Valley became part of Gatineau Park. Today, competing interest groups lobby for more change: horseback riding, rock climbing, ATV use, snowmobiling ... you name it, each user group asserts its demands. The argument usually is, "Gatineau Park is a public park. It belongs to us. Let us use it as we want."

But wait: who defends those who cannot speak? Who defends the rights of the trees that we love to see and the wolves whose howls we thrill to hear? How can we ensure, in our headlong rush to "experience nature," that we conserve the wild?

It is the fate of the National Capital Commission, guardian and keeper of the park, to juggle competing interests of users with the concept of wildlife refuge. Government downsizing of the 1990s has decimated, discouraged, and fundamentally challenged the remaining Gatineau Park staff. Yes, the NCC retains managerial responsibility for the park, but is the future of the park secure when consultants and contractors come and go? When cost-recovery is the mantra, and when tourism is perceived as the way to economic independence, is conservation truly a goal?

Some readers have remarked that writing a guide book encourages more penetration and hence destruction of the very wild places I love. But, whether or not I write this book, people will still head to the park to hike, bicycle, and swim in increasing numbers. It is my belief that the more knowledge we have, the more likely we are to care. Information gives us tools of understanding and helps us to unlock hitherto unseen, unappreciated clues about the world in which we live. Each of us can contribute to environmental protection. By keeping to the park's paths, not picking the wildflowers, and leaving behind only our footprints, we can make our own eloquent contribution to the preservation of Gatineau Park. Truly, the legacy is ours.

Former Prime Minister King, walking in woods near
Kingsmere, n.d. NAC PA–124444.

PART ONE

History of Gatineau Park

CHAPTER 1 ◼ The New Land: The Stage Is Set

> On the fourth day we passed near another river which comes from the north, where some tribes named Algoumequin [Algonquin] lived. It is not wide, but filled with a vast number of rapids, which are very difficult to pass. Sometimes these people go down this river to avoid meeting their enemies, knowing they will not look for them in places so difficult of access.[1]

In 1613 the great French explorer, Samuel de Champlain, set off from Montreal in the company of four of his compatriots and a "savage" in search of the Northern Sea. His journal records the above entry, which is possibly the first written description of the Gatineau River by a white European man. The French expedition was doomed to failure because of the treachery of Nicolas de Vignau, "the boldest liar" Champlain had ever met. Vignau claimed to have seen the Northern Sea (Hudson Bay) on a 1611 voyage up the Ottawa River, and had convinced Champlain that the Ottawa emptied into it, a journey he said they could complete in seventeen days. The thrill of exploration in their blood, the adventurers found not the Northern Sea, but a community of Algonquin at Allumette Island and the promise of expanded fur trade routes.

FIRST NATIONS' TERRITORY

The Gatineau region was important territory to Canada's Native people. At least as long as 6,500 years ago nomadic tribes used the Ottawa River as a trade route, extending from the Great Lakes to the Atlantic Ocean. Native copper implements (from copper deposits found particularly at Lake Superior in the Great Lakes region) have been found at both Morrison's and Allumette islands. Early people had settlements here dating from 6,000 years ago, according to the dating of found objects including bone needles as well as native copper tools. As well, river systems provided trapping access to interior forests. The confluence of the Ottawa and Gatineau rivers was no exception.[2]

When Champlain canoed up the Ottawa in 1613 he passed through "Algoumequin" (Algonquin) territory. This tribe summered along the Ottawa and during the winter split into smaller groups, heading into the protection of the woods. Although native life during this period is often described as being in harmony with nature, the realities were harsh. Winter snows were treacherous, mosquitoes and black flies a torment, and rivers were untamed. A tribe's livelihood was wedded to game such as moose, deer and rabbit. The myth about how "easy" hunting was back then becomes apparent as you come to understand the vast territories that game occupy: perhaps only four deer in an area of one kilometre. And, deer have acute hearing and are fleet of foot. Thus, Native people's prosperity was intimately related to the land: if game populations flourished, so would the tribe; if the prey was depleted, a band suffered. Harmony or not, survival of the fittest was the reality.

Algonquin allies in trade were the Huron; their warring partners were the Iroquois. In his diary, Champlain observed that although there was a variety of game in the area, the Algonquin had to be wary of other factions: "The region about is filled with all sorts of game, which often causes the savages to stop there. The Iroquois come there also sometimes to surprise them while they are making the passage."[3]

From the mid 1500s until the Iroquois Wars' peace treaty July 1701, skirmishes and all-out battles continued. The Iroquois vied for control of the Ottawa River trade corridor and later, when Europeans penetrated their territory, they battled with the Algonquin, Huron and others for the highly lucrative fur business.

Archaeological findings support Champlain's journal, for remains of native settlement sites have been found at the Chaudière, Lac Deschênes, Allumette Island and many other spots along the Ottawa River. There were no major settlements in Gatineau Park. This may be explained by two factors. First, the abrupt ridge of the Eardley Escarpment, forming the park's southern boundary, presented a natural barrier to easy access from the Ottawa River. Second, lakes were too small to support either adequate game or beach locations for major settlement sites. Instead, today's park was possibly only used as an occasional hunting or fishing ground. Although Ridge Road is considered by some to have been an old "Indian footpath," there appears to be no concrete evidence to support this popular folk tale.[4]

Nonetheless, in an undated, unidentified newspaper clipping in NCC files, the late historian Lucien Brault noted:

From 1636 to 1649, the Iroquois relentlessly pursued them [the Hurons], each portage became an ambush, the Chaudière Falls ordinarily being the last one. To avoid it, the Hurons or the Algonquins, their allies, often paddled up Brewery Creek ... or the Gatineau River as far as Chelsea, thence portaged to Kingsmere Lake through Aylmer and Lac Deschênes. Another portage trail was from Leamy Lake, on the Gatineau River, along the Mountain Ridge to Breckenridge.

EXPLORERS' LEGACY

The name of Gatineau Park echoes the era of fur traders, voyageurs and native peoples. Nicolas Gatineau dit Duplessis was a notary in Trois-Rivières. In the mid-1600s he explored the then-wild river now bearing his name to search for new trapping lands. Some say he drowned in the Gatineau River.

Samuel de Champlain is well remembered in the park. A lookout, parkway, trail, and even an ancient sea bear his name. The Champlain Lookout provides a superb view of the Ottawa Valley plain, once covered by the Wisconsin Ice Cap. As this glacier melted over 15,000 years ago, saline waters from what is now the Atlantic Ocean rushed in to create the Champlain Sea. Then the land rose, and the great watershed successively reduced to the Ottawa River's present drainage pattern. Little did the hardy French explorer realize his adventures would spark the imagination of park visitors over 300 years later.

Champlain brought Étienne Brûlé to Canada as a youth of seventeen in 1608. Brûlé soon became an expert interpreter. He spent his happiest years with the Algonquin and Huron First Nations peoples, learning their languages and exploring a vast territory. Brûlé preferred the company and ways of the native peoples to that of Europeans. In turn, he was not well liked by the Recollet priests who came to tame the "heathens." They considered his lifestyle to be an affront to both France and God, setting the worst possible example to the "heathen host" they intended to civilize.

Brûlé's end was no less colourful than his life. He shifted allegiance to England after their formal occupation of Quebec in 1629. Shortly afterwards he "went native" despite Champlain's warning that he would be despised and mistrusted by all sides as a turncoat. In the summer of 1633, Brûlé died at the hands of the Natives who, it is said, ritually tortured and ate him — a frequent fate for enemies. The lookout and picnic ground bearing his name survey the Ottawa River he explored by canoe in 1610, en route to Lake Simcoe with his Huron guides.

PHILEMON WRIGHT: VISIONARY SETTLER

The year 1800 saw a band of hardy pioneers wend their way through drifts of snow to settle on the northern shore of the Ottawa River at the junction of the Gatineau River. They came by ox-cart, travelling as much as possible on the frozen waters of the rivers, avoiding the deep snows of the woods. Philemon Wright, accompanied by his family and five other families, arrived from Woburn, Massachusetts, to tame the rugged wilderness. The forests rang with the sound of axes as they started to build what became Wrightsville, and then Hull (now Gatineau). The town soon thrived as a prosperous centre providing supplies for the steady stream of largely American settlers who followed closely on their heels.

Although Wright had initially come to establish a farm, he soon realized that the thin topsoil would not support anything but a subsistence livelihood, and his keen eye turned to lumber. In six short years the first load of squared timber floated down river to Quebec City. At its peak, Philemon's company employed 200–250 men annually and sent up to twenty rafts to Quebec each year.

TIMBER!

Outside events shaped the destiny of the Ottawa Valley. In 1803 Napoleon blockaded the Baltic ports from the British, who desperately required timber for the construction of ships for the Royal Navy. Suddenly eyes turned to the colonies of Upper and Lower Canada, and specifically to the tall stands of red and white pine plentiful in the valleys of the Ottawa and Gatineau rivers. With the assurance of a ready and guaranteed market, Wright and many others saw their ticket to prosperity before them. In the next few years, rights to the timberlands and river passages were hotly contested.

By the 1820s and '30s colonial timber was supplying over 80% of the British market. Of this, more and more was coming from the Canadas through the port of Quebec. By the mid-30s over half of the total colonial product came from the Canadas and was increasing. The export of Canadian wood to Britain reached a high point in 1845. That year 24 million cubic feet of timber and 7 million cubic feet of deals were shipped to Britain from Quebec. Of this, the largest proportion came from the Ottawa Valley.[5]

The easily accessible timber resources of the Ottawa River were used up by the 1820s. The Gatineau and the Lièvre rivers became the next source, despite the series of rapids that made transportation dangerous. By 1832 the Gatineau River was "the chief seat of the timber trade in the Ottawa River system."[6] Watercourses like the Lapêche and Meech creeks were important transportation routes where logs were floated down to the Gatineau. And sawmills such as Trempes' at Ste-Cécile-de-Masham on the Lapêche created pockets of industry among the hills.

Working logs using a winch and cant hook from the pointers, near Cascades on the Gatineau River, n.d. NAC C–22037.

Shanty life, hitching up the teams for the day, n.d.
NAC C–29821.

By the late 1850s the market had shifted. The industrial revolution of the Americas overtook Britain's demand for square timber and soon sawn lumber became the trade staple. The last raft of square timber travelled down the Government Slide at the Chaudière in 1908. This was more than just a little bit of history: built on the Coulonge River in Pontiac County, this raft had a crew of eighty men and carried over 150,000 feet of timber. Recognizing its dramatic significance, J.R. Booth not only organized the event but also sold tickets to folks who wanted to ride this historic crib down the slide.

Nonetheless, logging continued as a major industry in the Ottawa and Gatineau valleys, as it does to the present day. In 1899 the *Ottawa Evening Journal* published this filler: "Wakefield: A great number of men from here have already gone to the woods." Shanty life actually continued until the onset of WW II.

GATINEAU VALLEY PENAL COLONY

Perhaps thankfully, not all proposed uses of the Gatineau Valley were realized. From 1826–29 John MacTaggart was the Clerk of Works for Colonel John By's Rideau Canal project. MacTaggart proposed that the remote Gatineau would make an ideal penal colony. Convinced that convicts could be transported here at a tremendous saving to Great Britain, he thought that they would "be quite apart from the rest of the inhabitants of the colony, and it would be perfectly impossible for them to escape." He continued:

> A tailor once took into his head to run away from his master at Hull, and return to Quebec, the place of his nativity. He started early in the morning, took a canoe, crossed over the River Ottawa, and entered the wilderness on the opposite side. Day after day the poor fellow wandered in the woods, and found nothing to support life but a few wild raspberries. At last, on the tenth day of his desertion, he came out at the Rapid de Chats, about thirty miles from Hull, and quite in an

Charles Marchand and lumberjacks at a log jam on the Gatineau River, n.d. NAC C–22036.

opposite direction to that he intended to travel. The mosquitoes had feasted on him in a shocking manner; as, in passing through the thick woods the trees had torn off his garments, and exposed his almost famished carcass to the mercy of the merciless insects. He got back to the lapboard, and never thought of stirring away more.[7]

BRITISH EMIGRATION POLICY

Again the outside world intervened, influencing the development of the Gatineau region. The War of 1812 and the Irish potato famines of the 1840s nudged the British into re-examining their emigration policies. The War of 1812–14 made them rue the day they had permitted so many American citizens to settle in their colony. Defence concerns prompted the posting of a proclamation in 1815: free passage, one hundred acres of land, and supplies for the first six months were promised to those willing to emigrate. This resulted in an influx of Scottish, Irish, and English immigrants to Upper and Lower Canada. In 1818, two regiments posted in the St. Lawrence were disbanded and many of the men decided to settle the upper Ottawa River. The potato famines peopled the region with Irish settlers who hoped to eke out a better living in the New Land.

The lumber trade was inextricably related to settlement. Timber ships that delivered pine from the colonies to England and Ireland filled their empty holds with a living cargo of immigrants on the return route to Canada. Conditions were appalling and only the hardy survived the disease, overcrowding, and poor food on board.

Upon their arrival in Montreal, passengers disembarked to continue their voyage by various means of transportation. Many negotiated the route upriver from the St. Lawrence to Ottawa by cargo canoe, later by boat, or along muddy roads by carriage and cart. The prospect of settling as owners of their very own land must have encouraged them, but as these people travelled through the rugged bush surely some felt daunted. Early immigration officials' colourful inducements to emigrate, such as, "All you have to do to get sugar is to go out and chop it out of a tree,"[8] must have rung grimly in their ears.

Immigration statistics of 1841 in Hull show the following demographic breakdown: out of 210 total landowners: "115 (54.8%) were Irish; 32 (15.2%) American; 24 (11.4%) English; 21 (10.0%) English Canadian; 12 (5.7%) Scottish; and 6 (2.9%) French Canadian."[9]

Many of the Irish were farmers, but once cleared of its bush the land only supported subsistence farming. Farms supported mixed crops such as potatoes, hay, buckwheat, apples, vegetables (predominantly root crops, beans, and peas), and produced butter, cream, milk, honey, and maple sugar. As well, farmers bred and trained horses for lumber camps, and raised oxen, dairy and beef cattle, sheep, and pigs. Even the dogs worked, being hitched to butter churns. In the old days, everyone and everything earned their keep.

The timber industry was a year-round employer. During summer, farms produced food such as potatoes, peas and beef that would be consumed by shanty workers. Also, horses were bred, raised and trained for the work, hauling logs from the forest teams. Men left the farms before the freeze, returning home after spring break-up in March or early April. Many walked out; some went by horse-drawn wagon. In those early days, settlements were built up twelve miles apart, the distance a wagon made in a day. Meanwhile, the women ran the farms, minded the children, and kept the fire going (no mean feat for they were often "in the family way"). Shanties existed within what is now the park. One was at Lusk Lake and in 1966, John Cafferty recalled:

> They took out a million and a half feet, twenty thousand logs, one winter. The teamsters in the shanties used to get up at 3 a.m. Mick Dunne, reading the time wrong, had once got up and harnessed his team at 12:15 a.m. instead of 3 a.m. [There were] fun and good times in the shanties — always something to keep a man laughing. It was pitch dark at 3 a.m. they used to make flares to see by — a bottle of grease with a wick in it, struck in the snow. The logs cut in the Lusk Lake area were dumped into Harrington (Mousseau Lake). The logs were floated down to Alexander's mill on Meech Lake.[10]

Another shantyman, Richard Mulvihill recalled relishing the cook's Sea Pie:

> The cook would take a quarter of beef, frozen, slice off a huge thin shaving of beef into the pot, cover it with a layer of bread, then a layer of beef, to fill the pot — "cooked with plenty of salt, but none of this adding tomatoes and that kind of stuff!" The cook would shovel some hot sand onto the baking spot, and place the sealed pot on it, cover it with hot sand, and leave it overnight to cook [for] Sunday night, when the men came to eat it.[11]

Logs were hauled to the rivers and lakes, and piled on the ice to await spring break-up. Then the rushing meltwaters catapulted the logs downriver. In spring the men returned to their wives and children — and what a homecoming it must have been. Once home, the summer cycle of activities — planting crops, tending orchards and nurturing the wheat, oats and hay to feed next season's shanty horses and cattle — immediately commenced.

Who were the first Gatineau settlers, and where did they come from? Where did they settle, and how did they manage in their chosen home?

CHAPTER 2 ▨ Gatineau Settlers: At Home
Up the Mountain

THE REVEREND ASA MEECH

A Congregationalist minister, Asa Meech came to Hull in 1815 from
New England. Like Wright, he travelled along the frozen St. Lawrence
River by sleigh and oxen with his wife and family. For a time he
preached in the St. James Anglican Church in Hull, but by 1821 he
had received title to 200 acres at the southeast corner of the lake
which bears his name, in the midst of Gatineau Park. Rights to the
land were received from Philemon Wright who, by that time, was the
government land agent. In November 1823 Wright described the farm
as having: "one house, no barns, 24 acres cleared, six under cultivation,
15 horn cattle, 15 swine, 2 horses, 4 sheep, 20 days work on the road
in the settlement, no saw mills, no labouring men, $50 expenses on
the land."[12]

In successive years, up to his death in 1849 at the age of seventy-
four, Meech bought more property and increased the productivity of
the land substantially, growing such crops as wheat, peas, and potatoes,
and producing many pounds of maple sugar each spring.

Asa's personal history at first reads like a tragedy. His first wife
died in 1809 leaving him to look after six small children. He then
married her sister and fathered another five children. Somehow the
couple found the time and energy to move up to the Gatineaus with
their eleven dependants, but bad fortune soon touched Asa again. In
the spring of 1822 his wife and three youngest drowned in spring
meltwaters of Brewery Creek, Hull. The preacher took another wife,
Margaret Docksteader, who remained with him until his death twenty-
six years later. His union with Margaret produced yet another ten
children, one of whom, John Docksteader Meech, maintained the
original farm until 1901. History treats Asa kindly. He is described as

> a natural leader (who) seemed to possess an aptitude for
> administering successfully to the sick... Irrespective of creed or
> birth, without remuneration, this talented and consecrated

man served the community, preaching the Gospel, supervising the Sunday School and on weekdays, teaching school in Chelsea for many years. In the winter, with his family, he travelled by sled the five and half miles to Chelsea and in the summer covered the distance over the rough terrain by wagon.[13]

Today Asa's original house exists as the oldest surviving structure in the park, albeit dramatically altered both inside and out by a succession of owners. Currently it is leased from the NCC. Visit the graves of Asa Meech and his wife Margaret Docksteader at the Old Protestant Burying Grounds in Old Chelsea (see Old Chelsea Cemetery walk).

Oldest structure in Gatineau Park is Asa Meech's homestead farmhouse, now leased. Meech Lake Road, south side. 1971. NCC historical file. NCC 05.0081000.00160.

THE MOFFATT FAMILY AND PINK BROTHERS: PARTNERSHIP SETTLEMENT

In 1822 James, Charles, and Samuel Pink, accompanied by their sister, Isabella, her husband Alexander Moffatt, their children and his brothers, arrived in Montreal direct from Belfast on the *Alexander of Whitehaven*. A bateau took them up to Wrightsville where they wintered. In spring, Samuel and Charles returned to the old country, where their parents had remained. The brothers came back in 1830 and 1831, respectively. For a few years, James Pink worked in construction and helped to build St. James Anglican, the first stone church in Hull. Like many of the menfolk, he volunteered for the local Hull and Templeton Militia, which drilled on the Chaudière Green near the Eddy Factory.

In April of 1826, James started to clear a lot in the Gatineau hills. The Moffatts helped James to clear a small farm that they planted with one acre of potatoes and four acres of corn. In the fall a log homestead was erected: this became the first Moffatt house. James started to clear adjacent land, and his brother-in-law, Robert Moffatt, began to clear land just to the north.[14]

Because the land was rough, it was not uncommon for families to help one another to clear their first homestead. A condition of title — settlement duties — required that the land had to be cleared and crops started within a certain period of time. Felling the trees was not the major hardship; it was stumping that proved most stubborn. In addition, settlers had to earn enough money to feed and clothe themselves prior to the harvest of their first crop, construct a home to withstand the rigours of the long harsh winter, and manage childbirth, illness, and the loneliness of starting a new life far from the community they had left behind. All of this, coupled with the humidity and heat of Gatineau summers and the madness of mosquitoes and black flies makes one wonder how pioneers had the determination and courage to stay.

In 1830 the community up in the hills was large enough to require its own school. Members of both families participated in the "school-raising," much in the same manner as barn-bees, and

> when it was noted that no one had brought along any whiskey, the entire company sat down and waited until a good load had been brought from Symmes' Landing, now Aylmer. Once the whiskey had arrived, work proceeded rapidly and by nightfall the log structure was completed. Mrs. Alex Moffatt supplied

the meals on the festive occasion, the dinner consisting of pancakes and maple syrup.[15]

The group selected the Tabernacle as an appropriate name for the log building that became the community school and church.

Today the brothers are remembered by the legacy of the road and lake that bear the Pink family name. As well, on Vanier Road just south of Mountain Road, there's the Pink Cemetery. On the north side of the park in the subdivision off Mine Road (see Pink Lake walk) Alexander Pink's circa 1870 brick farmhouse still stands. The son of Samuel, Alexander was renowned throughout the Valley as a champion marksman, winning a gold medal from the government of Canada in 1884. A plaque dedicated to the Moffatt family stands in a clearing just north of Mountain Road on land originally settled by Alexander Moffatt. He died on March 31, 1832, when a tree he was felling crushed him: an all-too-common ending to a pioneer's life.

HOPE HOUSE — MEECH LAKE

The Lacharité family was arguably the first to homestead at Meech Lake — in fact the lake was often called Lac Lacharité. Johanna Lacharité married Patrick Farrell, who became a major landowner around Meech Lake. It was Farrell who built the first dam and sawmill at the lake — the dam that Thomas "Carbide" Willson was later to use for his generating station on Meech Creek. It was a Farrell who sold some of his land to the Capucin Fathers in 1900 for their Meech Lake Chapel. (See Meech Lake walks.) In 1914, the Farrell home was rented to a John Hope, who later purchased it in 1916. The Hopes cleared some land to create both a tennis court and a golf course. The home was renovated in 1922 and was eventually sold to the NCC in 1967.

Successful landowners or not, life must still have been rough, a roughness that is palpable in Johanna and Patrick Farrell's undated wedding photograph. The portrait probably shows them in their best "Sunday" clothes. Although photographs were becoming popular, people seem overly stiff and formal when posing because of long exposures of over a minute.

Meech Lake's Hope House was probably the Lacharité homestead. In 1923, François Lafleur wrote that James Lacharité gave his property to Patrick Farrell as a wedding gift:

M. François Lacharité maria une de ses filles à un M. Paddy Farrell à qui il donna tous ses biens. M. Farrell vécut au lac, faisant culture et chantier. Il payait ses employés en terre. Six mois de travail méritaient quelques cents acres de terrain. Un homme pour un travail reçut 300 acres sur le chemin du lac.[16]

Mr. François Lacharité gave one of his daughters in marriage to Paddy Farrell. Mr. Farrell lived by the lake where he had a farm and sawmill. He paid his employees with land. Six months of work merited a few hundred acres of land. For his work, one man received 300 acres on the lake road.

Wedding picture of Patrick Farrell and Johanna Lacharité who lived at Hope House. NCC file #05–0081000–00163.

The quote describes Patrick Farrell as a farmer, shantyman, and businessman-employer. One of the Capucin brothers, Père Alexis, wrote in 1900 that Farrell owned a pretty green cabin and prosperous-looking farm by the lake. Farrell must have done well to be able to build a dam, erect the first sawmill on the lake, and acquire a sizable acreage.

Farrell family at Hope House (prior to its 1962 renovation). Patrick and Johanna are seated on the porch; standing to their left is Jimmy Farrell with wife Edith O'Mara-Farrell with children Joseph and Mary; to the right is Jack Farrell.
NCC file #05–0081000–00163.

LAC MOUSSEAU (HARRINGTON LAKE)

A contemporary of Asa Meech was an Englishman named Joseph Hetherington. Unfortunately, when he arrived in 1816 his name was misspelled as Harrington, an error perpetuated in his land grant of 200 acres, Township of Hull, in 1827. (The Hetherington farm still exists on Mountain Road.) By 1851, his eldest son (also Joseph) was living on a farm at the northwest corner of Meech Lake. John, the second-eldest son, married Harriet, Asa Meech's daughter. Although they do not appear on the 1861 census, John and Harriet farmed the southeast end of what Eardley Township surveyor Driscoll again incorrectly termed "Harrington Lake" on his map of 1850. So it is that the Hetheringtons became Harringtons, a confusion that confounds historians today.

But Harrington Lake is also known as Lac Mousseau after yet another early settler. *The Ottawa Journal* of Saturday, January 13, 1973, reported that the first land grant around the lake was to David and James Maclaren (of Wakefield) in 1860. David sold the land to Louis Mousseau in 1867, who sold it to his son Charles in 1876. The property stayed in Mousseau possession until 1905.

The story of the lake's double name is one that speaks of the seemingly eternal conflict between political parties, as well as the duality of our French and English heritage. The 1959 *Hansard* records how Mr. Caron rose to ask which name the lake should officially take, claiming that as a boy he knew it not as Harrington but Mousseau, as did all residents of Eardley Township. The telling answer was that the change "was done when the Liberals were in power" — just the sort of tired old arguments echoed in the halls of parliament today. The resolution was that "Lac Mousseau" should appear *after* the name "Harrington Lake."

But time does not stand still. The Commission de toponymie du Québec reversed this in 1962 so that the lake would officially be Lac Mousseau (Harrington Lake). As of 1987, the lake is now officially known as Lac Mousseau (because the Commission considers names in parentheses transitory). Thus, politics sends heritage a-spinning.

NCC records suggest that by 1850 an Irish family named Flynn purchased John Hetherington's property and that in 1890 they sold it to Colonel William Edwards, the wealthy American lumber dealer who owned 24 Sussex Drive, which became the prime minister's residence in Ottawa. Two half-brothers from Michigan, W.A. Drum and W.L. Donnelly then enter the picture: in 1902 they built a sawmill at the foot of Lac Mousseau. By 1911 William Edwards owned it. When he died in 1921, his nephew, Lt.-Col. Cameron Macpherson Edwards purchased the Mousseau properties. He demolished the buildings, including the sawmill, and erected a country "cottage" here in 1921. Thirty years later the Government of Canada purchased the property and since 1959 it has been the prime minister's summer retreat. Diefenbaker publicly said he didn't want it, Trudeau loved it — and many park users decry its presence. Interestingly, the retreat itself is known as "Harrington Lake." Alas, poor Joseph Hetherington is bereft.

Sawmill (demolished) on site of prime minister's Harrington Lake retreat (Lac Mousseau). NCC historical file H14–363.

Between 1921 and 1951, Edwards attempted several agricultural ventures. For example, he started a fox and mink farm in an effort to stimulate a business for local farmers whom he rightly observed had a hard life on marginal land. He also had conservation in mind: in 1929, he persuaded the Government of Canada to turn his property into a bird sanctuary. Edward's ambition did not stop there: the NCC files reveal that in the 1930s, he and an Englishman named Major Imra experimented with prefabricated concrete post and panel technology for two barns. It was Edward's hope that such modular techniques would prove popular.

By 1951 Edwards and his friend the Hon. William Duncan Herridge had bought almost 4,000 acres of land surrounding Lac Mousseau. Herridge, an Ottawa lawyer, son-in-law to Prime Minister R.B. Bennett and ambassador to Washington, used what is now the prime minister's guest cottage as his summer residence. Many of Bennett's "New Deal" speeches were composed here at the lake.

There were others on the lake. An Irish family, the Caffertys built two homes here: the second one, built circa 1896, and sold to William Edwards in 1920 is today's Herridge Lodge. Herridge purchased it from Cameron Edwards in 1925 and used it as his winter cabin until 1960.

Colonel Edwards built his summer retreat on Lac Mousseau in 1921:
it became the prime minister's "Harrington Lake retreat" in 1959.
Cliff Buckman photo feature, n.d. (NCP 496).
From NCC historical file H14–363.

Finally, the story of the lake cannot end without mention of the 200-acre Healey farm, of the few remaining settler's homes left relatively untouched (albeit sadly derelict). Edward Healey came here from Tipperary, Ireland, and built the 1840 homestead. Grandson Stanley and his wife Dorothy left this original family farm in 1955, moving into the Gillespie homestead adjacent to the prime minister's summer retreat, where they were caretakers until 1976. NCC files record Stan's recollections of the Gillespie home; John Gillespie married Michael Mulvihill's daughter and settled near Meech Lake in the 1860s. In 1921 Gillespie had sold the house to William Edward's company, and it had been moved in 1926 to its present location bordering Lac Mousseau.

Although the Healey farmhouse can be visited (see Pine Road walk), public access is barred to the prime minister's Harrington Lake retreat. The 1959 amendment to the Official Residences Act set aside ten acres of land for the private use of the prime minister. Today both gates and RCMP officers bar what has been rumoured to be (a highly improbable) 4,000 acres.[17]

Stan Healey's father, Daniel Healey is on the right, circa 1910.
Daniel was the son of Edward, who built the Healey homestead farm
at Lac Mousseau (Harrington Lake).
NCC historical file H14–565.

A LEGACY OF NAMES

In the early 1820s a host of settlers came "up the mountain." Their
names linger on in the names of lakes, hills, and roads, though some
names alter with time. William Jeffs was the major landowner around
what was originally Jeffs Lake; today we know it as Kingsmere. Politics
affects name changes, too: today's Étienne Brûlé Lookout used to be
"Montcalm Lookout."

By the 1850s many other settlers of Irish, English, Scottish, and
French origin were eking out a living among the hills. Records show
these names: Paddy McCloskey, Michael Ryan, John Keogan, Garrett
Fortune, and Jerry Sheehan. Ryan and Bradley, another settler, were
tailors who travelled the countryside with their sewing kits, plying
their trade.[18] The McCloskey farm sat atop the ridge southwest of
Meech Lake. A ski and hiking trail now traces their old road which
once provided the main link from Meech to Mousseau lakes.

The road at Lauriault's Hill precipitously descended from Kingsmere
Lake to Mountain Road. There are scant references to "old man Lario"
who lived at the foot of the hill in the "The Hollow." He came from the

Blue Sea Lake area (east of the Gatineau River) and had a "stopping place in Maniwaki."[19] Lauriault's roadway provided the ridge-top settlers with their most direct route to Aylmer. There used to be a skull and crossbones at the top of the hill with the inscription "13 people killed on this hill." The hill's deadly reputation prompted its closure in September 1957.

Mulvihill Lake takes the name of John Mulvihill, who "came to Bytown in 1828 and clerked a long while for Colonel Burke, of the old Hundredth Regiment."[20] He also fathered a long lineage: Lauriault sold his property in the Hollow to Phillip Mulvihill, John's son. Phillip's son Michael married Julia Murphy, whose family lived by Kingsmere Lake. By 1906 Willy Murphy operated a popular inn at his Kingsmere home and in later years he drove the stage from Chelsea to Kingsmere, transporting summer residents from the train station to their cottages. In the 1920s former Prime Minister King purchased part of his Moorside property from Michael Phillip Mulvihill, grandson of the original settler. To make matters more confusing, along came Basil (Bud) Mulvihill. In 1948 Bud took a bulldozer and dramatically gouged out Mulvihill Lake (see Lauriault & Mulvihill Lake walk). This incensed King who, fearful that the dam and lake would dry up his beloved Bridal Veil Falls, promptly started litigation against Bud, who by that time had also built a cabin at Mulvihill Lake.

Joseph Lusk arrived in 1820 from County Antrim, Ireland, and settled in Eardley Township. The village of Luskville, Luskville Falls, Lusk Cabin and Lusk Cave all take his name (see Luskville Falls and Lusk Cave walks). An old township map reveals that "J. Lusk" owned a lot bordering both cave and lake: most likely this was a woodlot. Joseph built a log dwelling on the site of present-day Ghost Hill Farm, which is the 1880 stone house built by Isaac Lusk. Not only were names like Hetherington totally altered; names were commonly misspelled on maps: Lusk Lake appears as Lucks Lake. On an 1802 map of Masham, Wakefield, and Hull townships, the Gatineau River is "Gatteno." The most recent example is Meech, erroneously changed to "Meach," a mistake that thankfully is mostly corrected these days.

When surveyor Driscoll drew up his 1850 Eardley Township map, Lac Philippe appeared as Philip's Lake. Both a John and a James Philippe dwelt nearby, and in 1931 the Geographic Board of Canada altered the name to the present-day French spelling. (While John may have settled in Masham as early as 1846, it is the census of 1861 that shows his name on a farm near the lake.) Both John and James married French Canadians and by all accounts were bilingual, like most of the settlers in Masham. Another possible derivation exists: Philippe Gervais, who had property bounding both sides of the lake, may also be responsible for the designation, albeit due to his first, not last name. The jury's still out on this one.

Today there are few reminders of life up the mountain during the 1850s and 1860s, but Ethel Penman Hope wrote that it was "a jolly place to live ... the boys and girls were always getting up dances and other festivities." In reality however, life was terribly hard:

> The squatters and some of the poorest settlers seldom wore boots, unless to church or a private dance. On these occasions the boots would be carried till within sight of the church or house, then donned for the occasion. The orchestra at such dances consisted of the best voice. For a time after such a discovery the victim had nothing to do but sing himself hoarse — helped as he was too often by the old custom of carrying a bottle.[21]

In the mid-1800s, Masham settlers fashioned what "luxuries" they could from natural products. They wore wooden clogs called "sabots" and made candles from bear grease for home and mass. Bears were described as "swarming" in the hills along the Lapêche. More than one writer of the time mentions disease being the most cruel foe: diphtheria and pneumonia and even smallpox were too well known in these early days.

MOUNTAIN TRANSPORTATION

By the 1850s the mountain community was networked with rough roads. Settlers had to perform road duty, because townships did not take on the responsibility for road creation and maintenance until this century. Ridge Road provided the major route up the mountain. Other trails such as McCloskey and Lauriault provided connections to the track up to Meech Lake and to the Mountain Road near Aylmer.

But going "over the Mountain" to Masham was a major event. The Catholic Mission of Ste-Cécile-de-Masham, Diocese of Ottawa, was founded October 9, 1840, by Monseignor Ignace Bourget from Montreal. At that time, 25 families were living there, near the Lapêche River. While the county of Masham was founded on May 29, 1850, it was still remote. In a history of the Ottawa Diocese, Hector Legros wrote:

On venait ... par voie des lacs Meach [sic] et Philippe, en passant par Chelsea. Il n'y avait, à partir de Chelsea, qu'un pétit sentier qui permettait à peine à cheval de passer en portant son bât de farine et quelques effets essentiels. Ceux qui faisaient le trajet à pied devaient prendre la voie des lacs et se transporter en chaloupes. Combien rude était cet vie!

They came . . . by way of Meach [sic] and Philippe Lakes, passing through Chelsea. After Chelsea there was nothing save a narrow trail that allowed a horse to pass by, carrying a sack of flour and other essentials. Those who went on foot had to take the lake road and then go by boat. How primitive it was back then!

In 1855, Masham council received complaints from residents who clamoured for a road to connect them to the Ottawa River.

Roads were virtually impassable in the spring and wet periods. James Gillen lived two miles along the south shore of Meech Lake. He owned a horse and wagon, and often helped neighbours by giving them a ride to the village. Because the Meech Lake Road did not fully extend along the lake's southeast shore, the wagon was dismantled and taken to the foot of the lake by boat, to the present site of O'Brien Beach. It was reassembled and hitched to the horse that had been led by hand along the shore's edge. Once hitched, the wagon proceeded along the Meech Lake Road to one of the Chelseas or perhaps to Ironside or Hull.[22] It was several years before Tom Gillen cut the Meech Lake Road beside the south shore.

The main mode of transportation was by "shank's mare" (foot), for only the more prosperous settlers could afford a horse. Typically a trip to Hull and back took two days. Two days seems short to us: men who made this journey often carried 100-pound sacks of flour or other staples across their shoulders. The necessity arose not only for proper roads and modes of transportation, but also for inns where tired travellers could rest.

Who knows how it started — perhaps a bolt of lightning, perhaps stump-burning gone out of control — but flames ravaged the mountain on August 17, 1870. Apparently the conflagration began on the Ontario side of the Ottawa, jumping the river near Breckenridge, just below Ghost Hill. In two terrifying hours the fire swept a two-mile strip over the mountain to Ironside. The town was razed and homes of the fifty iron miners were destroyed. Families fled — and some never came back. Others did return to pick up the pieces of their lives and start over. Not a single home had been spared. As a result of the 1870 fire, subsequent fires of 1915 and 1923, and the logging operations, the stands of pine on the mountain exist no more. They have been replaced predominantly by mixed hardwood forests.

Tales of the 1870 fire abound in the quaint local history of Anson Gard in his circa 1906 journal-cum-history, *Humors of the Valley*. The tales are fraught with self-conscious humour, but are worth repeating to give a sense of the severity of the damage as well as the good-natured spirit of the settlers:

> Why, it was that hot that the apples roasted on the trees a half mile away from the edge. At first we thought this a total loss of the fruit, but, bless you, it turned out a great saving, for all we had to do was to pick and barrel them apples, and all winter long we had roast apples and cream for breakfast, and cream and roast apples for dinner, and didn't once have to bother wasting wood to bake 'em for supper. I never, before that winter, had had enough baked fruit, but I was real glad when long toward spring we finished the last barrel, and haven't hankered for baked apples since.[23]

The old man who spun this tale evidently was just warming up, for he continued with other lavish stories. Although the facts were grim, only two people are said to have lost their lives:

> An old man and an old woman were suffocated. The daughter of the former saw the danger and, quickly gathering her children and father, started for the Mountain Road, reaching which she turned to the east, but by this time the fire, coming from the west, had so gained upon them that they were soon caught by

the suffocating heat. The father fell from the buggy, but the brave daughter got out and lifted him, now unconscious, back, and again tried to beat the fire, but the race was too uneven. All about swept the hot, blinding smoke, and yet she raced on and on, her strength fast leaving her, and yet she would not give up. Again her father fell from the buggy, but this time to his death, for his daughter had no strength to lift him up.

The story continues, telling how the daughter and her children were saved by her "noble horse," although her mother died after returning to the homestead to try and save the farm animals. During the following mild winter, Gard reports that the government provided tents for the needy who could not rebuild their shacks, and generous townsfolk provided money and supplies.

By 1914 many of the settlers had left the hills, the rights to their land having been sold by auction. The land was not considered valuable: the thin soil, the barrier of the Eardley Escarpment and the rocky outcrops combined to make it largely unproductive for agricultural purposes or attractive for settlement. The harsh life is alluded to by Herbert Marshall in his book, *History of the Ottawa Ski Club*. He describes one of the early settlers, John Dunlop, who had a log cabin up the hill near Camp Fortune: "a hardy pioneer who, at the turn of the century, gave up the fight against bears, trees and shrubs and moved his house and wares down the valley."[24]

Some families lingered on until after WW II, when the economics of the times dictated that subsistence or local market farming was no longer viable. It is during this time that most of the land beside Lac Philippe was purchased by the NCC.

CHAPTER 3 ◙ Industry Among the Hills

THE WAKEFIELD MILL COMPLEX

The Lapêche River tumbles down from the hills in its descent to the Gatineau River at the present site of Wakefield. The site was perfect for the construction of a mill, which proved a catalyst to the further development of the area. As it expanded under the management of the Maclaren family, the mill complex provided sawn lumber, hydroelectric power, and woollen goods to the burgeoning community.

In 1838, William Fairbairn petitioned Sir John Colborn, Governor of Upper and Lower Canada, for permission to erect a mill on the site, which "is a place destitute of mills ... being twenty-four miles from a grist mill."[25] Settlement was increasing in the region and there was a demand for a mill where people could grind their grain. Fairbairn was granted his request and promptly built his mill. Six years later, in 1844, he sold it to John and James Maclaren for £300. Local history is fraught with rumour about the conditions of sale. Sources suggest that Fairbairn only sold his mill under the influence of alcohol — alcohol that he was encouraged to imbibe by the Maclaren brothers themselves ...[26]

The Maclaren family has a long association with the Gatineau. In 1824, David Maclaren, a successful merchant and businessman, set sail from Glasgow, Scotland with his wife, Elizabeth Barnet, and their three sons, James, John, and Henry. They initially settled at Richmond, Ontario, where David, William, and Alexander were born, prior to the couple purchasing land and moving to Torbolton. David Maclaren set up as farmer and schoolteacher there. In 1840 he left the farm to Henry's management and moved the family to Wakefield where they immediately made their impact as entrepreneurs. The J. Maclaren Company Limited is still in operation today.

John and James entered into partnership to purchase the Fairbairn Mill, borrowing the required capital from their father. During the years 1844 to 1861 they expanded the operation to include a sawmill, woollen mill, brickyard, and general store, as well as homes for the various mill workers. The sawmill was erected on the east side of the river, below the large brick house which still remains. The circa 1860 Maclaren house was probably built by David Maclaren for his two sons, James and John. It seems John and his wife, Georgina Baird, lived here and it is possible that James did too, before he moved to Buckingham. (Sometimes the home is called the Bachelors' House.) Today it is part of the Wakefield Mill Inn complex.

James Maclaren, n.d.
Collection of Dr. Stuart and Norma Geggie.

Although Fairbairn's original mill was intended to service the immediate market, the operation expanded under the brothers' management to service the lumber shanties up the Gatineau River. James Maclaren's interests and acquisitions in the lumber business prompted him to move to Buckingham, Quebec, in 1864. John Maclaren became a silent partner in James Maclaren Co. Ltd., preferring to remain in Wakefield to run the mill complex. The Buckingham office of the company became one of the Wakefield mill's main customers. From that village, a variety of goods including oats, peas, beans, and woollens were sent upriver to the shanties for the long winter months.

In 1868, John Edmond walked from Torbolton Township to Wakefield, to begin forty-three-year's of service as miller at the mill. Wakefield Village historian A.B. Robb writes of an amusing incident:

One day, a farmer, who must remain anonymous, brought his wheat to the mill to be ground, just as Mr. Edmond was about to go to dinner. He explained to the farmer how to tend the machine, so the flour would not overflow the container, and left for his noon-day meal. The farmer, his grinding done, bagged his flour and also left for dinner.

Some time later he returned, complaining that his wife couldn't use the flour, "it got as hard as a stone when she added water to it." A little investigation by Mr. Edmond revealed that the customer, left alone, had slyly added to the brown flour some white substance from another barrel nearby, believing it to be some of the coveted new style flour, and that he could improve his mix at no cost to himself. Unfortunately for the schemer, the lovely white "flour" was not flour at all, but some plaster of Paris which Mr. Edmond was using to repair the grinding stone.[27]

Maclaren's General Store was another successful enterprise in Wakefield village. By 1900, it had grown from humble beginnings as a log house to a thriving rural store selling groceries, clothing, and dry goods. Woollen material made at the mill was retailed here by the yard, and a dressmaking and millinery service was available for the creation of ladies' clothes. The shop was not only a retail outlet: from 1848 to 1912 it housed the post office and served as a bank, offering 3.5 percent interest compared to the 3 percent offered in the city.[28] When the farmers came to the mill delivering their sacks of grain to be ground, their womenfolk sometimes accompanied them, making an outing of the event. The excuse for a get-together, the prospect of a new dress, or window-shopping, each must have been a big draw.

A succession of fires swept Wakefield, the first in 1877:

Maclaren's grist mill and woollen factory with contents were burnt this morning. The fire originated in the factory from a paper of matches that had by some accident got into a sack of wool and ignited while passing through the machine. The loss is not yet known but supposed to be in between $15,000 and $30,000. The fire is still raging on the hill behind the village.[29]

The Maclarens rebuilt; by 1881, the mills were back in production. In 1892, the first train arrived at Wakefield, linking the village to Ottawa, Hull, and across the Gatineau River to Buckingham. Western wheat was now brought by rail to the mill for grinding. By 1900, Alexander Maclaren had succeeded his father James as head of the company. Under his hands the mills were modernized and rollers were used instead of millstones to grind the grain. Installation of a generator brought electricity to the village. A new-found prosperity touched the village.

Maclaren's mill and complex on the Lapêche River, Wakefield, circa 1865. NAC C–18612.

On May 17, 1910, disaster struck again. A major fire gutted the entire complex:

The Ottawa Fire Brigade sent an engine, eight men and 2,000 feet of hose under the supervision of Captain Bradley but they were too late. The loss to fire was 5,000 bushels of wheat, 2,500 tons of oats, 900 bags of flour, a large quantity of buckwheat, 900 bags of shorts and bran, and 200 cord of firewood ...

The fire spread to the forested hills, and for a time it was feared that the village was threatened, thus necessitating the arrival of another detachment of the Ottawa Fire Brigade and the powerful engine "Victoria" to help douse the fire until it was quenched by rain the following day. As a result of the fire, 30 men lost their jobs and the damage was estimated from $50,000 to $60,000.[30]

Although the gristmill was rebuilt on a grander scale, the woollen mill and sawmill were not. In 1939 Alexander Maclaren passed away, and with him died the production of flour. J.P. Henderson bought the mill: he stripped it of much of the machinery and converted part of the building to apartments lit by the mill's own generator. In the 1950s brothers Kenneth and Ernest Young leased the mill, first from Henderson and then from the NCC after its purchase of the property in 1962. The brothers repaired and reassembled the machinery, producing animal feed until their retirement in 1980.

THE FORSYTH AND BALDWIN MINES

The same John MacTaggart who thought the Gatineaus would make an ideal penal colony recorded that an iron deposit was discovered in 1801 with the deflection of a compass needle. The discovery innocently started over a century of speculation, arguments over land claims, and excavations of a variety of mineral sites.

In 1826, Philemon Wright formed the Hull Mining Company and arranged for Louis Akey to homestead on the lot, perform the required settlement duties, and mind the property. Major removal of ore was not attempted, however, until Tiberius Wright sold the mineral rights to Forsyth and Company of Pennsylvania in 1854. Until that time only a few excavations had been made to support local needs. The 1855 Paris International Exposition featured a one-ton iron ore sample from the mine.

Part of the problem was setting up an adequate transportation system that would take the ore to market. It was a problem that beset the new owners as well. The mine now began to produce:

In the late summer of 1855, 13 men and 3 horses were quarrying ore at a rate of 1,300 tons a month. About 15,000 tons were shipped between 1854 and 1860. The ore was loaded in boats on the Gatineau River, shipped across the Ottawa and through the Rideau Canal, and reloaded on lake vessels at Kingston for transport to Cleveland and from there distributed to various customers in the north-central United States.[31]

The mine was fated to change hands again and was sold to the Canada Iron Mining and Manufacturing Company. At this time a blast furnace was built at the current site of Ironside on the Gatineau River, but the devastating fire of August 1870 razed the village, destroying the furnace. Afterwards the mine went up for sale, advertised as "11,100 acres of wild lands for sale on advantageous terms."[32] Local lumber merchant and iron founder, Alanson H. Baldwin, purchased it. Although the mining was primarily done by hand, steam equipment was used for drilling while dynamite was used for blasting.

Baldwin took advantage of the fire's devastation to prospect the nearby lots. He purchased land from the Pink family and opened a second mine, the Baldwin Mine. Two large piles of ore appeared at Ironside, waiting for transportation by George Chaffey and Brothers of Kingston. It was shipped down to Kingston by barge, transferred to lake schooner and taken through the Welland Canal to Cleveland, Ohio. "During the Baldwin regime (1871–1874) shipments from the Forsyth Mine probably amounted to 35,000 tons and the Baldwin Mine 3,000 tons."[33]

However, Baldwin had not cleared title to his land, so in the mid-1870s he suffered from many legal actions. He was no sooner rid of settling title when 420 tons of ore from his mine was seized and held on a lake schooner, the *Clara Youell*. The case was tried in Toronto in June 1877; Baldwin lost his claim to the ore. The mine never fully recovered operation after the legal troubles, although some ore was mined during the 1950s. Although the Forsyth mine shafts can still be seen near Mine Road, the NCC does not maintain the site.

In the park's southwestern sector, near Quyon, molybdenite was mined. Used in the production of steel, it became an important commodity during WW I. The Moss Mine opened in 1914 and represented the first commercial production in Canada. From 1916 to 1919 it was the world's largest producer, shipping 0.75 million tons during WW I. The village of Quyon prospered during this time.

Forsyth Iron Mine, circa 1860. NAC C–3522.

Mica was also mined extensively in the early 1900s in what is now the park: one such mine was at Pink Lake and others dot the landscape along "Mica Mine Trail."

Moss (Dominion Molybdenum) Mine, Quyon, 1917.
NAC C–22964.

THOMAS "CARBIDE" WILLSON: A WORLD'S FIRST AT MEECH LAKE

The ruins at Meech Lake are no secret to those that know Gatineau Park, but the story of the fellow who built them, Thomas "Carbide" Willson, is not as well known.

Born of United Empire Loyalist stock on a Princeton, Ontario, farm in 1860, young Thomas Willson knew a different kind of hardship to that of the pioneers. In 1865 his father lost the farm and a few years later died, leaving his wife to rear their two sons. The family moved to Hamilton, where Thomas' mother taught Spanish guitar, painting, and took boarders to put her two boys through school. Thomas never forgot his mother's support. Years later he built her a home in Woodstock, Ontario.

Throughout his lifetime Willson was a tireless and ingenious inventor, engineer, entrepreneur, and electro-chemist, fascinated with the emerging technologies of his day. At twenty-one he applied for his first patent on a "dynamo electric machine," an arc light which supplied Hamilton with its first electricity. Even at this time in Canada's history, the "brain drain" to the United States was occurring. Unable to find a firm offer of employment in Canada, Willson accepted a position in New York. During the next few years, he took out a variety of patents for many different discoveries.

Thomas "Carbide" Willson, his eldest son and wife, Mary (née Parks), circa 1909. NAC C–53483.

While experimenting with aluminum, he discovered how to produce calcium carbide, a product which was to make his fortune and extend his influence to international proportions. He sold the American patent to what became the Union Carbide Company in the United States. By 1895 the American, British, Canadian, and Australian markets were controlled by the syndicate, and Willson had patents in forty other countries.[34] Fearful of losing the rights to the Canadian market, he rushed back to Canada in 1896 to build his own carbide-generating plant in Merriton, Ontario, which turned a profit for him even in its first year of operation.

The man was tireless. Willson owned iron and steel patents so that he could make machinery for his many industrial plants, and by 1900 he owned all rights to produce hydroelectric power on the Saguenay and Shipshaw rivers in Quebec. By 1904 he owned the patent and many plants for acetylene production, and had a contract with Sir William Van Horne for lighting railway carriages. He developed an acetylene gas buoy, thereby winning a contract to light the St. Lawrence River.

Although driven by an enquiring mind and competitive nature, Willson was a rather stiff, formal man. Evidently his genius did not extend to interpersonal or social skills. However, when Mary Parks came up from California to study the piano at the home of mutual friends, she entranced him. Seven years of diligent courtship proved successful, and in 1895 the pair were married. In 1901 they moved to Ottawa to be close to the seat of political power in Canada. Willson purchased a home on then-prestigious Metcalfe Street where they entertained the day's political leaders and prominent members of society. The young Prime Minister King was among those who enjoyed the sumptuous balls for which Mary Willson was renowned. Here in Ottawa, Willson

spent more and more time in the basement of his Metcalfe Street home, working in what he considered was the best-equipped laboratory in North America for the scientific investigation of nitrogen — the field that had started to command his attention. He viewed his nitrogen research as more important than his discovery of calcium carbide and he took out patents on his findings. He delved into the ways nitrogen could be used in fertilizers (ignoring the scepticism of the farmers of the day) and it was during this work that he decided to build a summer residence that later became his research headquarters.[35]

The Gatineau Hills beckoned, being a perfect location adjacent to Ottawa, yet secluded and tranquil. By 1904, Willson had installed an acetylene plant at the Gatineau Fish and Game Club on Thirty-One Mile Lake (east of the Gatineau River), which illuminated the club house until the 1930s.

After renting a cottage on Meech Lake and studying its water courses, he purchased land along the north shore. In 1907 he started building a half-timbered, two-storey, gabled summer house with two wood furnaces, seven fireplaces, and eleven bedrooms — all using local materials. Private telephone lines were brought in from Old Chelsea so they would not be isolated from business interests and social obligations. A large fish pond was dug and Mary had a small orchard of apple, pear, and plum trees planted in addition to a flower garden. Apparently Willson owned Ottawa's first automobile — and then its second and third. "He was too nervous to drive himself, so it was necessary to have a chauffeur. At least one of the cottagers at the Lake was driven in to Ottawa to the Hospital where her baby was safely delivered, though with holes like bathtubs on the Chelsea Road it is hard to imagine."[36]

By 1909, he had purchased 460 acres at an average cost of $22 per acre. This included all of Little Meech Lake and the start of Meech Creek just at the waterfall where Patrick Farrell had built his dam. The couple found the Gatineau Hills soothing. Despite her renown as a hostess, Mary did not enjoy crowds or the hustle and bustle of city life. Husband Thomas was delighted to spend most of his time working in his laboratory furthering his studies of nitrogen. Encouraged by others who said his fertilizer was so revolutionary that it would put every other fertilizer company in North America out of business, Willson decided to build a plant at Meech Creek:

In 1911 Willson built a dam on Meech Creek using 1,004 bags of cement, four or five railway carloads. In the next two years he put up a power house. This was a hundred thousand dollar experimental station. He was proud of the acid tower he built and believed it to be a perfect acid condensation plant, the first Phosphoric Acid Condensation Plant in the world.

No sooner did his experiments commence than the summer residents at the Lake were up in arms. One day their boat houses would be six feet under water, then they would be six

"Carbide" Willson's powerhouse and dam, under construction, circa 1913. NAC C–53492.

feet from the water. He wrote Mrs. Mary A. Tilley on June 19, 1912, that he would arrange her boat house so that it would be comfortable no matter what height the water might be.[37]

Willson was convinced that the fertilizer plant would be an overwhelming financial and industrial success. He sold his other companies and took out loans against his patents with a single investor, American tobacco king J.B. Duke. His financial dreams then turned to nightmares. Duke absorbed all the assets when Willson's time limit for production ran out.

Although the Meech Lake plant fell into disrepair, Willson himself was not totally ruined. His interests in Newfoundland were not included in the Duke deal: he turned his attention to developing that province's hydroelectric capacity. In two years he formed another twenty million dollar corporation — but alas, in 1915, while seeking additional venture capital, he collapsed on a New York street, dying of a heart attack.

The acid condensation tower, dam, and generating plant were never maintained. The tower fell victim to a fire, and now only its base remains standing. The dam and the generating plant — windows sadly gaping — still stand to haunt the cascading waterfall with memories of industry. Willson would surely be shocked to realize that "The Mill," as his plant is erroneously but affectionately known, is a popular spot for nude sunbathing. (Be forewarned, hikers: the ruins are well worth exploring regardless of this creative use of scenery.)

The house still stands, but it is barred to public access, being the federal government's conference centre at Meech Lake. In 1923 it was sold to A.J. Freiman, the Ottawa department store owner and in 1938 to Ottawa dentist Joseph Gilhooly, who sold it in 1979 to the NCC.

CHAPTER 4 ◪ Recreation Up the Mountain

To think that we have been in and around Ottawa for more than two years and yet no one has told us of this Mountain Road, and we so near it and so often. It just makes me feel like scolding at these Canadians for being so silent about all the grandeur by which they are surrounded.[38]

The grandeur about which American author Anson A. Gard wrote in 1906 was not the main reason for the initial settlement and industrial development of the Ottawa-Hull and Gatineau region. But it was a significant incentive for some of the later residents who chose this land for their country retreats and summer cottages.

THE IMPACT OF TECHNOLOGY: THE TRAIN AND CAR

By the turn of the century, improved roads and the opening of the Ottawa and Gatineau Railway in the 1880s permitted easier access up the west side of the Gatineau River. In February 1901 the Interprovincial Bridge was built, linking the railway from its most northerly terminus at Maniwaki to Ottawa. The hinterland was opening up:

By 1900, more than 60,000 passengers and 24,000 tons of freight were carried over the line. The company owned 2 engines, 2 first class passenger cars, 8 excursion cars, 1 second class car, 2 baggage, mail and express cars, 6 cattle and box cars, 21 platform cars, 1 conductor's car, 1 snow plough and 1 flanger.

The trip from Ottawa to Farrellton cost $1.15 in 1892, but three years later, first and second class fares were introduced and the price actually dropped so that a first class ticket cost $1.20 (75¢ second class) while a trip from Ottawa to Gracefield cost $2.05 ($1.50 second class).[39]

Time creates the illusion of inexpensive fares. But rail was not within reach of the ordinary labourer, who worked a six-day week at wages of $1.25 for a ten-hour day.

Nonetheless, increasing numbers of people could afford the train and also its later companion in transportation, the automobile. In 1907 a Model T Ford cost about $900, making it a luxury item when we consider the labourer's wages. New-fangled gizmos or not, cars were often viewed as a hazard, especially on country roads: "They scared the wits out of weaker-hearted citizens and the daylights out of placid horses. The farmers alleged that they scared their pigs, killed chickens, caused cows to dry up and drove their women into hysterics."[40]

Chelsea Station, circa 1914. NAC C–42930.

Despite the considerable voting influence of the farming community throughout the nation, the automobile was here to stay. Thanks to its increased penetration of the countryside and resulting development of both gravel and "Macadamized" roads, people enjoyed the luxury of independent travel. In combination with the railway, former remote countryside and lakes became accessible to city-dwellers for all types of recreation.

Imagine the scene: a calm summer evening, the stars twinkling overhead, the Milky Way tracing through the heavens, the smell of the pine and the kiss of the breeze on your face. You are beside the dark waters of Meech Lake and your mood is mellow with the night. Suddenly your senses are alert: the sound of singing floats across the lake, starting on the breeze and ending gently, leaving you waiting … waiting for another song. So it was in the early 1900s at Meech Lake, when the Capucins would canoe to the middle of the lake to serenade the stars — and the cottagers — with hymns they sang in French.

The Capucins are an offshoot of the Francescan Order and came to Canada from France in the year 1890. They established a church at 20 Fairmont Avenue in Ottawa, being part of the St. François d'Assise parish. The Order required a summer retreat for their students, especially those suffering from tuberculosis. And, in 1900, Père Alexis discovered a perfect location:

> *La bonne Providence me conduisit sur les bords du lac Meach [sic] ou villégiaturaient quelques Pères Dominicains de nos amis. Le lac me séduisit; je découvris au fond d'une baie un joli promontoire boisé d'une superficie de quatre arpents, propriété d'un fermier irlandais du nom de Farrell, impropre à la culture, mais idéalement adapté au but que je me proposais.*[41]

> Providence led me to the shores of Meach [sic] Lake where several Dominican Fathers lived. The lake seduced me: I discovered a beautiful wooded promontory of perhaps 4 acres alongside a bay. It belonged to an Irish farmer named Farrell. The land was unsuitable for cultivation but ideal for my purpose.

Farrell sold Père Alexis the land on the point on the condition that the Capucins permit his elderly mother to attend Sunday Mass with them, rather than having to go all the way to Old Chelsea. The conditions were acceptable. Soon a chapel and a cottage were constructed. Another writer, François Lafleur, commented that many of the cottagers attended the Mass.

> *"Rien n'est plus beau, en effet, que de voir, tous les dimanches matins, 25 à 30 chaloupes se détacher du rivage pour se diriger*

vers la maison du Seigneur. Souvent des protestants s'y joignent."[42]

 Nothing could be more beautiful, really, than to see, upon every Sunday morning, 25-30 little boats ply the lake's waters to the chapel. Often Protestant worshippers attended too.

Both writers mentioned the confusion over the name of the lake, stemming from one of the original settlers. Lafleur recounts that François Lacharité lived at Meech Lake in 1849:

M. François Lacharité a longtemps donné son nom au lac Meach. Etablis à peu près en même temps que M. Meech, mais comme riverain et cultivateur, les sauvages, les bûcherons, les trappeurs le visitaient et retournaient en disant: «Nous venons du lac Lacharité» tandis que les ouailles de M. Meech répétait... «Allons au lac Meach...» mais ici le vocable anglais supplanta le français.[43]

For a long time, Meech Lake was known as Lac Lacharité. François Lacharité was living there at approximately the same time as Asa Meech. He was a riverman, and cultivated a garden by the lake, too. The French loggers and trappers who visited him would say, "We're off to Lac Lacharité." But at the same time, English speaking people would say, "We're going to Meech Lake." It was the English name that became dominant, so the lake became known as Meech Lake.

The chapel continued to serve all of the Meech Lake cottagers, becoming an institution during the summer months. By the 1940s there were over 150 families living on the shores of the lake, and the little chapel could not accommodate them all. In 1956 a second was built, paid for in two years at a cost of $8,500. A huge, carved wooden statue stands outside the chapel. Father Bernadin of La Fraternité des Capucins told me it depicts Saint Anthony, a Friar Minor who was one of the first followers of Saint Francis. It was carved by Victor Tolgyesy, a Hungarian immigrant. The NCC now owns this property and leases it to the Order.

Father Bernardin also related how, as a twelve-year-old novitiate, he used to walk to this chapel from the Ottawa church. The brothers always left at midnight, walking along Wellington, crossing the Ottawa River on the railway bridge (Alexandra), and then walking to Mine Road and

Old Chelsea, to Meech Lake. Once on O'Brien Beach he would wave his arms in the early morning light until someone picked them up in a boat and deposited them at the Chapel. The trip took five hours.

COTTAGE COUNTRY AT MEECH AND KINGSMERE LAKES

At the turn of the twentieth century, it was fashionable to have a summer residence. In the late 1800s, cottages sprung up along both Meech and Kingsmere lakes. NCC files describe the W.J. Tilley summer residence built beside Meech Lake about 1870–72:

> *Dans le passé, la cuisine était une cabane complètement détachée de la structure principale. … il fallait servir la nourriture par la fenêtre à l'aide de plateaux. Le chalet principal comprenait donc un salon, trois chambres à coucher et un étage supérieur. Son toit avait été fait de bardeaux. Il y avait un hangar pour la glace, un cavot creusé dans le sol pour la viande, un jardin potager, des fleurs et un emplacement réservé au jeu de croquets.*
>
> *… vers les années 1900, on y organisait le service de la messe avec un pasteur d'Ottawa et d'autres voisins. Quand ce n'était pas possible un père Capucin dirigeait alors la cérémonie.*[44]

In the past, the summer kitchen was constructed in a completely separate cabin from the principal structure. A little window conveniently allowed trays of food to be passed through. The main house had a living room, three bedrooms and an attic. Its roof was made of cedar shingles. It had an ice house, meat cellar, vegetable and flower garden, and a space on the grass reserved for croquet games.

… Around the year 1900, Mass was organized and led by a priest from Ottawa and many neighbours attended. Whenever he was unavailable, a Capucin Father led the ceremony.

Years later, in 1930, John Ambrose O'Brien commissioned Ottawa architect W.E. Noffke to build his summer estate up at Meech Lake, close to the mansion of Thomas Willson. His father, Michael John O'Brien, spent fourteen years building more than eleven Canadian railroads, including the section of track called the Crow's Nest Pass. Under the father's direction, the family businesses grew to encompass shipbuilding, and gold and coal mining in both northern Ontario and Quebec. M.J. O'Brien was appointed to the Senate in 1918 and died in Renfrew in 1940. J.A. O'Brien expanded his father's business interests into construction, smelting and refining, and dredging in the Great Lakes. He lived at 266 Clemow Avenue in Ottawa and died in 1968. O'Brien Beach on Meech Lake is named after this family.

In the 1870s Sir John G. Bourinot purchased land for a summer retreat from the farmer named Jeffs who, by 1863, owned nearly all the land surrounding Kingsmere (formerly Jeffs) Lake. In fact, it was Sir John, along with Colonel Dennis and H.V. Noel, who instigated changing the name of the lake. Arthur S. Bourinot, the poet and son of Sir John, wrote: "Father bought the Jeffs' property in the seventies, and did over the old log farm house, which looks very much the same as it did when I was a boy. My father had large orchards, grew excellent grapes, and, of course, kept a horse which was a necessity."[45]

Getting to cottage country was not easy in the 1900s. Bourinot continued:

> Our family usually spent three or four months there, depending on the House of Commons, of which my father was clerk. The day of the move, we hired a moving van to take extra furniture, more particularly the piano, which my mother played beautifully, pigeons and a dog and various other articles. The van, pulled by horses, left early and usually arrived about lunch time.

> The family drove their own horse in a buggy or carriage. There was, of course, a train and William Murphy drove the stage to Chelsea. His forerunner was a Mr. Shean who sold his place to the Murphys and it was eventually owned by Colonel Wattsford. It is now torn down. If you were taking the stage, you listened for the horn blown by Billy Murphy at your gate, who drove you to Chelsea station. You then took the train to the old Broad Street station in Ottawa, and from there took a street car up town.

Today there are many houses crowding both Kingsmere and Meech lakes. The Meech Lake residential community comprises roughly eighty-two cottages and year-round homes — and more seem to be erected every time I drive past. Sixty-three are on the south side of the lake and nineteen are on the north side, accessible only by boat. The 2000 NCC Master Plan suggests twenty more lots could be built upon. According to the 2000 *Gatineau Park Parkway Sector Plan*, at Kingsmere Lake there are currently 71 homes west of the parkway overpass with sixty-four permanent homes and seven cottages. Approximately thirty to thirty-five more homes could be erected if subdivisions are allowed.

Both areas are considered Special Management Zones. Certainly, many homes predate the creation of the park. However, their existence offers challenges to the NCC who constantly juggle public and private interests in Gatineau Park.

THE HERMIT OF KINGSMERE

Arthur Bourinot was a gentleman poet who found inspiration in the secluded woods and glades up the mountain. He wrote a narrative poem, "The Hermit," that weaves a romantic tale about Miles Barnes, who lived near Kingsmere Lake. Both "Barnes Road" and a path named "Hermit Trail" are named after the recluse.

William Lyon Mackenzie King visits Miles Barnes, "the hermit," near Kingsmere, n.d. NAC PA–124443.

It was the late Ed Ryan of Old Chelsea who identified the bearded figure in this National Archives photo as Miles Barnes. Known as "the hermit," he stands at the door of his ramshackle cabin, gun in hand. I will never forget how this photo prompted a gasp of recognition — and a story to share — from Ed.

Ed told me that Barnes was a reclusive soul who kept much to himself in his modest shack. He kept dogs, perhaps for company as much as to warn him of the uninvited company of visitors or curious children. A map prepared by Ed and Lid Ryan in 1965 from the 1875 valuation roll of the Municipality of West Hull shows the property of Miles Barnes nestled among other neighbours such as Timothy Moffatt and Michael McCloskey. His home was surrounded by an orchard of apple trees which, it is said, can still be seen by those who know where to look. The trees supplied the fruit he peddled about the countryside to earn the cash for staples.[46]

Ed Ryan remembered the hermit staying at his parents' home, being fed and kept warm one cold and bitter winter. Neighbours were concerned about the old man, and Ed's father decided to head up through the snow by sled to check on him. He was alone in his dilapidated, cold shack. All he had to eat were the apples saved from the autumn harvest. William Ryan brought Barnes to his farm — apparently it took some persuasion.

By and by the time to be leaving arrived, but Miles Barnes was in need of greater care than he could manage on his own. At that time, the Grey Nuns operated St. Patrick's home on the corner of Laurier and Kent Streets. William Ryan travelled into the city to inquire if the hermit could be accommodated. The sisters agreed, and it was here, at St. Pat's, that Miles Barnes soon died.

And so the tale seems ended. But not quite, for while researching Gatineau-related poetry one day, I stumbled across Arthur Bourinot's poem "The Hermit." The opening paints a picture of Barnes' cabin:

> We came upon the clearing suddenly.
> Its beauty stopped our feet and motionless
> We stood; it caught our breath, the unceasing white
> And pink of apple trees in Maytime bloom
> And then the dogs were on us, with bared fang
> And angry snarl they harried us until
> A voice called them from the door of a small house
> We had not seen before and in the doorway

Loomed and grinned a huge and bearded man whose bulk
Like that of Atlas holding the heavy earth
Supported on his shoulders his small home.
He spoke, the dogs slunk off, their bellies low,
And we went forward then to meet our host
For we had found the hermit in his wood.[47]

Bourinot's sentimental and romantic poem is evocative of the feeling of Miles Barnes' life. In contrast, Ed Ryan recollected his father's concern for the hermit and distinctly remembers Barnes' presence in his home.

Bourinot was a great supporter and friend of both Duncan Campbell Scott and of Archibald Lampman, two Canadian Confederation poets. Apparently Lampman's poem, "Heat" — studied by Canadian school children — was composed while the poet walked up Mile Hill to Ironside. Duncan Campbell Scott's "Last Night a Storm Fell on the World" was written at Kingsmere, possibly while staying at Deepwood, the Bourinot property.

MACKENZIE KING: KINGSMERE RESIDENT

The Bourinot family name is inextricably woven into another Gatineau Park notable: former Prime Minister William Lyon Mackenzie King. Arthur Bourinot tells this story:

> King bought his first property from my mother in 1902. And in 1903 he built his first house, which still stands and is now owned by the Canadian Government. My home, Deepwood, part of the Jeffs' farm is next door. I can remember as a boy seeing Mr. King carry his old mother down the hill to the lake where he would sit with her in the evenings, and then carry her back up the hill. No small feat as anyone who knows the slope can testify to.[48]

Today the NCC operates King's first house, Kingswood, as a historic site. Each summer the cottage, boathouse and outbuildings are open to the public as a museum.

King first saw Kingsmere Lake while on a bicycle trip on Thanksgiving Day, 1900. After purchasing the land, he built Kingswood in 1903. He often invited his parents there, and it was during his mother's last year of life in 1917 that he used to carry her down the steep hill to the lake. This is the memory Bourinot recalled. King also built an ice house and in 1923 a garage, to house his government car. Proximity to the lake aggravated his sciatica, so in 1924 he purchased more land, this time from the Herridges. He named it Moorside, calling the field adjoining the house the "moor."

King pictured himself as an English country squire. At Moorside he created extensive gardens and also reconstructed a series of stone "ruins." This collection came from buildings that were being demolished both in Canada and abroad. In 1941, King made a particularly embarrassing request of Lester B. Pearson, then a counsellor at Canada House, our High Commission in London. King had just heard that the Palace of Westminster had been bombed. Could, King urgently asked, Pearson just get some stones and ship them over? Pearson obliged but the collection only arrived at Kingsmere in 1947. The enigmatic King never incorporated them into his Abbey ruins.

Arthur Bourinot coloured King's land with mystery when he wrote:

There was once what we boys called a haunted house at Kingsmere. There was one part of it standing. It was located just below where the King ruins now are. You can still see the rows of old maple trees which the early settler planted around his home. We used to play there and looked upon it with awe. It is now all gone and covered up; even the foundation; but the maples are still there. There was supposed to have been a murder there, so the legend goes.[49]

King loved nature. But his was a romantic notion: not for him the natural vista of rock, stream and wood. Instead, he determined to tame and "beautify" nature. We can observe this in his diary entry dated September 9, 1924:

During the day I had Paddy and Willy Murphy remove the barbed wire from around the Moor cottage, it was a joy of joys to see the larger vistas opened up and the fine stretches of lawns. The weeds of course were much in evidence in the lower reaches but they will be cleared off in time. There is no joy comparable to that of redeeming the waste places, making the desert to blossom like the rose whether it be in the wilds of nature or in the vagaries of human nature.[50]

Along with his friends Godfroy and Joan Patteson and his crews of workmen, King carved trails out of the bush surrounding Moorside. The waterfall found just to the south of Moorside on the Lauriault Trail was one of his favourite destinations, to which he took such notables as Winston Churchill. His ultimate intention was to create a pathway suitable for a car, with bridges spanning the brook. His diary chronicles the building of the waterfall trail:

> At 9:15 despite rain which had just stopped but still threatened and which came down fairly heavily about 10:30 for 15 minutes, I went into the woods and worked with Armstrong underbrushing and clearing up by the stream. Willy Murphy with the two horses (Jess and Dick) and two men had taken away most of the heaps of brush collected during last two days and several of the fallen trees ... We worked at underbrushing till about 12:45. There are some beautiful bits by the stream and we are making the worst slashed place look like a park.[51]

The "worst slashed place" refers to the clearing of the woods for the sake of firewood. One of the factors motivating King to purchase more and more land for his estate was the devastation of the woodlands. He remarked that his neighbour Charles Fleury had "ruined the appearance of the property as a forest. It breaks one's heart to see anything so lovely as this woods might be, being mutilated in this way."[52] Earlier on, in 1924, he said of his purchase of Moorside, that: "It will greatly increase in value in a few years, but the value will depend on other properties being kept away. There is always danger of trees being cut down, small lots sold to undesirable people, as campers being given permission to pitch tents nearby, leave tins and papers about."[53]

Whether he is judged as conservationist or snob, King increased the size of his estate to nearly 500 acres prior to his death. King's will reveals the deep love he felt not only for his Kingsmere properties, but also for the people of Canada. He had a very real sense of obligation to his electorate, exhibited here in his will of June 24, 1950:

> It has always seemed to me that the highest joy in life is to be found in some form of public service; that instead of the State being indebted to the one who gives of his time and means to the country's affairs and to the betterment of human conditions,

the obligation is the other way round; where the opportunity of public service is given, one cannot be too grateful to the source whence it arises.

I had not been long in office before I conceived the idea of acquiring sufficient land to make the Kingsmere properties into a park which would be worthy of its location in the immediate vicinity of Ottawa, and which some day I might present to my country as a thank-offering for the opportunities of public service which the people of Canada have given me. If I have been able to carry on in the service of the State for the length of time I have, I shall always feel it was due in no uncertain measure to the enjoyment I have derived from developing these properties over the years, and having simultaneously in mind their ultimate presentation to the people of Canada as a public park.[54]

Canada's tenth prime minister was a family man who never married. He loved his parents, brother and sister, and was devastated when they all died within six years. His closest friends were Godfroy and Joan Patteson, who shared his love of country rambles, gardening, and good conversation at Kingsmere. Stories linger on about his interest in spiritualism and mediums, and of his long conversations — and political consultations — with his Irish terriers Pat I and Pat II. Coupled with his reverence for the land and his generous bequest to the people of Canada, such tales tell of a complex, imaginative man. As you wander the woods and meadows of his dreams at Kingswood and Moorside, perhaps you will see his tweed-clad figure striding down the trail …

INNS UP THE MOUNTAIN

Père Alexis' description of the land surrounding Meech Lake in 1900 is interesting because of its objectivity. He writes of abandoned farms, overgrown clearings, and stumps left from logging. The impression is one of desolation. Amid this scene, Père Alexis discovered Meech Lake to be a beautiful oasis, a silvery lake bordered by trees. With the exception of the pretty, light green Farrell farm, he observed that there were few other dwellings, save perhaps two or three dozen cabins hidden among the trees. But for those who could negotiate the rocky road by foot or stagecoach, Meech Lake beckoned as a quiet retreat into nature.

Evidently he was not the only one who perceived its tranquility. It was a good spot for an inn. No surprise then, that in his 1927 description of the long walk from Old Chelsea to Meech Lake, Père Alexis mentioned a rustic inn:

> *"Et voilà comment après une heure de marche laborieuse, on parvient à une auberge rustique, refuge de citadins en quête de fraîcheur. On est sur une éminence; et en bas, tout proche, un coin de lac Meach apparaît."*[55]

And so, after an hour of laborious walking, one came upon a rustic inn, a refuge for those seeking refreshment. It was on a little rise, and behind it, very close below it, you could see a little corner of Meach [sic] Lake.

This was Meech Lake House, formerly the (Thomas) Cowden House, which had served as the Meech Lake Post Office. The Alexanders

Meach [sic] Lake House, n.d. Note the three cars sporting windshield signs "Alexander's Cars to Meach Lake."
NAC C–38477.

operated the inn (later on, the O'Briens purchased it for their staff and, after they sold it to the NCC, it was demolished). Emma and Andrew Alexander were married on September 22, 1908, at Beachburg and then moved to Meech Lake. Andrew Alexander worked for Gilmour's Lumber Company for a while, and it was he who built the first sawmill on the lake. In turn, Emma soon became renowned for her cooking. At their home she fed not only her husband's mill employees but also the schoolteachers who taught at the little Meech Lake school. Many of the teachers boarded with the Alexander family.

In 1914 the Alexanders moved to the hill overlooking the lake and started Meech Lake House Hotel, in the former Cowden home, where Thomas Cowden had operated the Meech Lake Post Office. (Unfortunately, this structure befell the same fate as many others. It was demolished by the NCC after its purchase from the then-owners, the O'Brien family.) But Meech Lake House prospered with the Alexanders:

> In the early days there were few cars on the gravel roads of the Gatineau, but as far back as 1915 Andrew Alexander owned three touring cars which he personally kept in condition and these he used to meet the daily train at the Chelsea station, almost six miles away, to transport the visitors to Meech Lake House. He had Johnny Dunn of Old Chelsea and Edmund McCloskey to drive the cars as well as himself …

> In those days, keeping summer guests comfortable and happy was no easy task. Food was rationed and there was no electricity, running water or telephones. But this spacious rambling old home, with Mrs. Alexander as its kindly hostess, was, from its opening day, filled to capacity with summer vacationers who revelled in the swimming, boating, tennis and hiking amid the beauties of the picturesque Meech Lake. Guests would arrive as early as May and the last ones would end their holidays by October.[56]

Keeping food fresh in the hot summer months before refrigeration was not easy. Ice from Meech Lake was stored in sawdust at Hope House. There is many a reference to the cutting of ice on Meech, Philippe and Harrington lakes. Ice was cut using long saws, loaded onto horse-drawn wagons and hauled to the underground ice-houses.

During winter, the Alexander's home, as well as several establishments at Kingsmere such as Murphy's Boarding House, the Mountain Lodge, and the Candlelight Tearoom (at the corner of Kingsmere and Swamp roads), were popular spots for skiers to find a hot meal, good conversation and rest.

Cutting ice for summer's ice house was a winter job. These men are on the Ottawa River, but others would have been cutting ice on Meech, Kingsmere and other lakes., n.d. NAC PA–8932.

DUNN'S HOTEL

Four hotels, all operated by Irishmen, jostled for business in Old Chelsea in the late 1800s. One was Dunn's Hotel, the present-day Dawn House, opposite Scott Road, on the Meech Lake Road. The original dwelling was built in the mid 1800s by Josiah Chamberlin who built a sawmill and gristmill on Chelsea (formerly Brook's) Creek for Thomas Brigham. In 1875 John Dunn built an addition, transforming the former private home into the Dunn's Hotel. In 1900 it burned, to be rebuilt and covered in pressed tin by Henry and Billy Fleury.

Dunn's was a popular stopping place for the teams of men and horses that logged by Lac Mousseau. It continued as a hotel and popular drinking spot until the temperance movement of 1907 ended the

Dunn's Hotel, Old Chelsea. John Dunn is in the lower centre, leaning against the post; Mrs. Dunn is 5th from left on the top verandah. The old schoolhouse where Asa Meech preached and taught is at the far left. (It burned in the early 1900s.) NCC historical file #05–0081000–00112.

John Dunn and his wife Anna Grimes, with children, circa 1890. NCC historical file #05–0081000–00112.

serving of spirits at the inn. Subsequently, Mrs. Dunn operated both a post office and store here until 1920.

Behind it is the Old Chelsea Cemetery where you'll find the graves of Asa Meech and his wife, as well as those of Emma and Andrew Alexander, innkeepers of Meech Lake House.

THE OTTAWA SKI CLUB

In 1910 the Ottawa Ski Club was formed, based first of all at Rockcliffe Park and then at Fairy Lake, its major purpose was to encourage ski jumping. However, as early as 1907 there is a reference to night skiing by torch light at Fairy Lake.[57] It was not until after the First World War that cross-country skiing really took off as a sport, although locals such as the Alexander family were apparently avid skiers. Andrew Alexander made the family skis, fashioning them himself out of hardwood and using leather cut from fittings at his mill for the bindings.

The push to encourage cross-country skiing really began in 1913 thanks largely to the efforts of C.E. "Mort" Mortureux, who began cross-country races starting from Murphy's Boarding House at Kingsmere (on present-day Booth Hill) and terminating in Rockcliffe Park. After the war, cross-country touring of the Gatineau region became extremely popular, and such towns as Kirk's Ferry, Ironside, Kingsmere and Tenaga became linked by a trail network. The distances the skiers covered and the extent of the trail building is well documented:

> On Saturday, January 19 [1919] a ski-party set out from Ironside via the Mine Road and stayed at Murphy's in Kingsmere overnight. Sunday morning it crossed the mountain to Kirk's Ferry, taking the Dunlop Hill and Cooper's Hill on the way. It met another party which had arrived at Kirk's Ferry by train and led them back over the hills to Murphy's for a noon meal. At 3:30 p.m. it left for Ottawa via Pink and Fairy lakes and arrived at the toll-gate at Ironside at 5:30, having covered in all 30 miles during the week-end.[58]

Ever-increasing numbers of skiers frequented inns up the mountain. Between 1920 and 1932 several lodges were built in the area. Some, such as Pink Lake and Western Lodge, were moved at least once. In 1920, the Ottawa Ski Club purchased its first land at Camp Fortune —

incidentally buying the best land for downhill skiing, which became more popular than cross-country skiing in the 1930s. The land included an old woodcutter's shack that the Club promoted as its very first lodge. Camp Fortune took its name from the settler Garrett Fortune.

In fact, settlers gave their names to many of the lodges of the Club. In 1923 Keogan Lodge was built:

> Keogan's clearing (to use the name left by the original settler many years ago) has long been known to skiers and others who have roamed the Gatineau Country, as one of the most delightful spots of this nature in a district noted for scenic beauty. On a small knoll in about the centre of this old-time clearing and surrounded by half-grown pine and spruce, rests what is now known as Keogan Lodge. The clearing itself is about 150 acres in extent and is formed of gently rolling slopes and knolls... The ski trails from Wakefield, Cascades, Kirk's Ferry, Chelsea, and Kingsmere all converge at this point, and the run leading from Dunlop's Farm on the Meach Lake Road passes directly over Fortune Lake.[59]

Kirk's Ferry, 1925. Disembarking skiers from Ottawa preparing to ski to Camp Fortune. NCC, Gatineau Park slide collection.

The lodges all were connected by a network of trails, cut and maintained by the dashing Night Riders and Trail Riders of the Club. It was common for both men and women to ski at least twenty miles in a day. Women soon forsook their feminine attire and "beat the men at their own game" as they adopted pants as the *de rigueur* outfit for greater ease and comfort. Trails took on names that were at once descriptive, historical or simply picturesque: "Nightmare Trail," "George's Trail," "Nature," "Hermit," and "Petticoat Lane" to name just a few.

Once again, technology of the day stepped in to change the availability of the countryside to the city-dweller. The age of the bus started to overtake the train in 1924, and the emphasis of trail-making adapted to a new shift in population concentration. Instead of people coming to Tenaga by train, for example, they were now whisked from downtown Ottawa or Hull up to Kingsmere Lake by bus. The fare was 30¢ from the corner of Sussex and George streets in Ottawa to Old Chelsea; for an additional 15¢ the skier could get right to Kingsmere Lake. In 1928, the Club announced in its newsletter, *Ski News*:

> May we again remind our friends, the owners of the motor cars, and those using taxis, that this is the first time in the history of skiing that an attempt has been made to keep the road open as far as Kingsmere. The road, however, is too narrow to provide double lines of traffic. The Gatineau Bus Company is unable to push the snow any further on account of the fences and it simply means that a bus running from Kingsmere meeting a car coming from Old Chelsea must both go into the ditch. There is no remedy for the situation at present and skiers motoring to the hills will be well advised not to go any further than Old Chelsea.[60]

Of course, penetration of so many into the countryside was not without its problems. Western Trail, originally cut by the author of the *History of the Ottawa Ski Club*, Herbert Marshall, caused a fuss with the landowner who claimed damages to his bush lot because the trail was cut so wide. But it seems that problems were the exception rather than the rule, and most were amicably resolved, often through the negotiating skills of another of the Club members, Joe Morin. It was the same Joe Morin who, in 1932, opened Slalom Hill, the first downhill run.

The Ottawa Ski Club was responsible for developing the Gatineau hills for lovers of nature and sports enthusiasts alike. It was the Club that was instrumental in starting the Federal Woodlands Preservation League. For a time, its honorary president was none other than King, a natural liaison born out of a shared love of the land and an ardent desire to preserve it. *Ski News* of December 24, 1930, described how one had to "pick your way through a ragged bad lands of stumps, all the woodcutters left of a noble pine bush" in order to get to another trail.

CHAPTER 5 ❖ The Park Is Born

> I hereby bequeath to the Government of Canada as a public park in trust for the citizens of Canada … my several properties at Kingsmere, in the Province of Quebec, amounting in all to nearly Five Hundred (500) acres, and the houses and other buildings erected thereon.[61]

William Lyon Mackenzie King wrote the above-quoted words in his will of 1950, hoping to ensure that his beloved Moorside would be preserved and enjoyed by the public in perpetuity. His acreage represents only a small portion of the 35,600 hectares (88,000 acres) contained in Gatineau Park. In fact, the Park was created through the concerns and pressures of many individuals and associations. Recreational users of the land were among the most active conservationists and continue to be the most ardent of the Park's defenders today.

As guardian of the Park, the NCC struggles with three major and often conflicting mandates: conservation, interpretation, and recreation. As urban sprawl encroaches on its boundaries, the Park is increasingly viewed as a local playground and tourist destination. Some say that it is already a "zoo," being one of the few places we the public can experience nature and wildlife. As population densities increase, the public makes more demands upon its resources.

The NCC is an easy scapegoat: their task, quite frankly, is that of a juggler. For the NCC must balance the preservation of the ecologically sensitive park with our recreational wants. It is perhaps not surprising that there has been a succession of Gatineau Park Master Plans as the years go by, as new needs and sensitivities have evolved. But how did the park come to be?

THE WASHINGTON OF THE NORTH

In 1884 Sir Wilfrid Laurier observed that "Ottawa is not a handsome city and does not appear to be destined to become one either." As if to thwart this pronouncement, the Ottawa Improvement Commission (OIC) was created in 1899 during his tenure as prime minister.[62] (It was the first of a succession of federal government bodies that in 1958 culminated in the NCC.)

As the name suggests, the mandate of the OIC was the enhancement of the city itself. Under its jurisdiction Ottawa urban planning began in earnest with the landscaping of the canal area along with the maintenance of Rockcliffe Park and the planning of city squares and parklands. Montreal architect Frederick Todd was hired and in 1903 tabled a report advocating the creation of a park adjacent to Ottawa. In 1913 the Holt Commission under the government of Sir Robert Borden echoed his stand.

However, the recommendations were shelved. The country descended into austerity with the advent of WW I. In 1927 the Federal District Commission (FDC) replaced the OIC. The marriage of this organization to the dreams of King and other individuals and associations (like the Federal Woodlands Preservation League), gave birth to the political commitment that sparked the creation of Gatineau Park.

FEDERAL WOODLANDS PRESERVATION LEAGUE

Concurrent with the bureaucratic and political manoeuvrings over the Park's creation, concerned citizens urged government purchase of Gatineau lands. The Federal Woodlands Preservation League was born out of the concerted efforts of the Ottawa Ski Club, among others. Honorary presidents were two of our prime ministers: King and R.B. Bennett. Not incidentally, both men were bewitched by lakes. King loved Kingsmere, and Bennett found tranquility at Mousseau. In his report of 1903, Frederick Todd advocated measures to control the destruction of forests by the woodsman's axe. Warnings were ignored.

Firewood was a major catalyst precipitating the creation of Gatineau Park. During the Depression of the 1930s, farmers and jobbers clear-cut the bush lots for a dollar a day. (Ironically, many a cord was hauled to Parliament Hill to heat its cloistered halls.) The result was an increasingly spotty landscape of small farms, stripped woodlots and secondary growth hardwood forests that were replacing original, harvested stands of red and white pine. A 1935 report of the Department of the Interior entitled "Lower Gatineau Woodlands Survey, Interim Report, Ottawa 1935" commented on the devastation:

Wood dealers in Hull and Ottawa ... purchased the entire timber stand on a woodlot outright from the farmer ... The purchaser ... is concerned only with the maximum volume of fuel wood removable and the faster it can be out the sooner will returns be obtained. In practice cutting is usually let by contract to sawmill jobbers who operate the year round on the basis of payment of so much per cord. These jobbers believe that it is to their interest to cut every stick acceptable for fuel wood, in consequence of which the entire area is stripped of every tree over one inch in diameter.[63]

The report analyzed the potential harvest of the forest under sustained yield production, noting natural disasters such as fires that swept the area in 1870, 1914, and 1920 and their resulting damage to topsoil. But the report concluded that, when considering the region as a *whole*, logging *could be sustainable*. In terms of yield, a ½ cord per acre, per annum was typical, with an overall yield for the region being "6,000 cords under sustained yield management."[64] Because approximately 4,000 cords were cut in what is now the park "it cannot be said that cutting from the area, as a whole, has been excessive. The weakness of the present practice is in the irregular distribution of the cutting which is concentrated in certain sections resulting in denudation of these areas, while at the same time timber on other sections is becoming overmature."[65]

Thus the combined forces of natural and human-engineered "patchwork" devastation left a hardwood forest of varying maturity. No level of government enforced any reforestation. Why? Because the rights of private ownership, and inertia at all levels of government, prevented the encouragement of sustainable production. The report recognized the dilemma: "In view of the fact that all the lands in the area are privately owned, the problem of instituting a system of management whereby cutting would be carried out under a selection system is complicated. Private owners cannot be expected to forego personal gains or returns for the general public benefit."[66]

The recommendations of the Federal Woodlands Preservation League can be loosely grouped under two broad categories: that of continued but selective logging under one of a variety of control mechanisms, or the purchase of land for the creation of government-controlled parklands.

By the late 1930s, the federal government was being pressured on all sides to make a decision. Various interest groups lobbied for and against a park. But ever in the background was prime minister King's vision …

JACQUES GRÉBER — MASTER PLANNER

King first met architect and urban planner Jacques Gréber in Paris in 1937. Gréber came to Ottawa to meet with him about the development of a long-term master plan for the capital and its environs. The creation of Gatineau Park figured prominently in their minds. It symbolized Canada, with its outcrops of rugged Precambrian rock, sylvan lakes and woodlands.

But outside influences dictated the turn of events. World War II, along with the varied interests of the FDC, prevented a park from becoming reality. Gréber and Canadian planners John M. Kitchen and Édouard Fiset formally proposed the creation of Gatineau Park; despite this, the proposal known as the Gréber Plan was not completed until 1950. It was tabled and passed in the House of Commons under the government of Louis St. Laurent on May 22, 1951.

LAND PURCHASE AND EXPROPRIATION

Meanwhile, the Federal Development Commission (FDC) had been granted approval to start purchasing land in 1934. In 1938, the acquisition process began, and by the start of WW II, 16,000 acres were under its control at an average cost of $10 per acre. But some property owners got far less: the lowest I've noted is $4.50 an acre in 1949. However, in 1956 land payments had been reviewed:

> The amount paid for land by the commission has been much more reasonable since 1953. However, the damage had been done by the earlier agents of the FDC in threatening the landowners with legal complications if the FDC offer was not accepted. This has been the basic reason for the lack of cooperation experienced today from the remaining landowners.[67]

In the 1950s, Gréber encouraged the purchase of more land to accommodate future needs of a burgeoning population as well as to complement the capital's beauty. By 1956, the FDC had accumulated "about 50,000 acres of the planned park area of 75,000 acres."[68] Most land purchases happened in the 1950s and '60s. At that time the parkways were constructed, and in 1963 and 1964 the Willson and O'Brien estates were purchased, adding 706 acres to government holdings. In 1964, Asa Meech's house was purchased, the oldest structure in the Park.

Stonemasons building the retaining wall for the Étienne Brûlé Lookout (formerly Montcalm Lookout), Champlain Parkway, September, 1956. NAC PA–163906.

But the problem for the government was that these holdings were not contiguous. And, as improvements such as the parkways were built, market value of property skyrocketed, resulting in acquisitions being increasingly costly. Charges of conflict of interest were rampant as people perceived there was one rule for the poor, another for the rich. There seemed an all-too-ironic lack of political will to enforce parkland purchase among the wealthy and influential residents of

Kingsmere Lake, an issue that was hotly debated in 1956 — and beyond. In the 1970s, emotions exploded as the Societé d'Amenagement de l'Outaouais (SAO) expropriated land in the Meech Creek Valley. Yet again, homes were demolished and barns razed to make way for a much-touted zoo that nobody seemed to really want. What ensued was a different kind of zoo, one of rancour and frustration. Today, no caged animals pace the tranquil valley, but residents still recall that bitter time. Until 1994, the Meech Creek Valley was still owned by the SAO. During that year, the NCC and SAO completed a land swap and "the Valley" became part of the Park.

Today, when I'm in the Park, sometimes I come across a solitary soul standing by a clearing, staring in silence or even weeping. It makes me reflect: creating and managing a park fosters a terrible conflict. The public (you and me) demand a park and access to its haunts, but individuals are loath to relinquish their treasured homes to public access. It's a sticky morass.

Among all these conflicting interests, there is a far larger issue at stake. Who defends the wildlife? Who believes in and defends the concept of sanctuary?

HERITAGE BUILDINGS: PUBLIC CONCERN

NCC files reflect the public concern over the fate of buildings inside the park boundaries. The Meech file contains an assessment, noting that Asa's house could be permitted to "rot gracefully" as it did not possess "any historical value." However, public pressure helped to save this home: it still stands, albeit much altered. During the 1960s the Gatineau Valley Historical Society lobbied for its preservation, and there was talk even of making it a museum. An NCC memo dated June 25, 1969, reveals the NCC's change of attitude about Meech's 1821 homestead: "… we should endeavour to have this house preserved using Historical Development funds. Even if it costs $15,000 to make it habitable, I believe it should be saved from rotting. There are few enough historical buildings in the National Capital Region in Quebec to deliberately permit their destruction."[69]

Other Kingsmere properties didn't fare so well. The historic J.R. Booth mansion was demolished after a bolt of lightning struck it. And in 1973, a cottage called Shady Hill, part of King's bequest to the people of Canada, was torn down despite a public outcry.

Thomas "Carbide" Willson's home overlooking Meech Lake, where
the Meech Lake Accord was not signed!
Photo dated July 13, 1917. NAC PA–144966.

Let's be fair. By 1973 preservation and renovation became the new
aim of the NCC, partly in response to public pressure. The *Ottawa
Citizen* quoted an NCC official as saying that "the best way to save
two decaying cottages on King's estate would be to find a public use
for them."[70] Today Kingswood Cottage and Moorside are beautifully
restored for public education and use.

It is true that most of the old pioneer dwellings are lost. McCloskey's
farm is only remembered by the trail bearing its name and a sepia
photo in an out-of-print book; the Hermit's hovel simply decayed in
the woods, victim to time. Stan Healey's historic farm cries out for
preservation, as does Adrien Martineau's complex of buildings near St-
Louis-de-Masham. The Maclaren brothers' house still overlooks the
Wakefield Mill where the Lapêche River tumbles over the falls. Once
operated as a summer museum by the Gatineau Valley Historical
Society, both structures are victims of NCC cutbacks and their fate
remains unclear.

Who knows what tomorrow will bring?

PUBLIC ACCESS — OR THE LACK OF IT

Although still standing, the Willson and O'Brien mansions are government retreats that are banned to the public. There is rumour that O'Brien House might be turned into a trailhead hotel, or bed and breakfast. The Farm, private residence of the speaker of the house and part of King's bequest to the people of Canada, is not open for us to view.

But perhaps the greatest outrage on the part of park users centres on the prime minister's summer residence on Lac Mousseau (Harrington Lake). Woods and lookouts, trails along Pine Road near Herridge Lodge, and even sections of the lake itself are guarded by electronic sentinels, signs and barricades. No-nonsense RCMP officers turn people away if they approach too close to the grounds, specifically along the old road to Mousseau and Philippe lakes or Masham along the Meech Lake Road. Long-time public-access advocate John Almstedt says that RCMP have ordered hikers, canoeists, and artists to leave Lac Mousseau.

It seems an absurd joke: what is celebrated as a public park paradoxically contains not only private homes but also residences reserved for the exclusive use of politicians who are paid by the public. NCC staff awkwardly dance the dance: on one hand they speak of public access, on the other try to justify the legacy of elitism. For those of you who wish to pursue this, look up the *Hansard* of June 16, 1959. It records the then-unanimous approval of the creation of a summer residence for the prime minister. On that day, Mr. Leduc rose to address the house:

> Personally, I am very pleased with the government's decision and I can assure the house that the people of Gatineau Riding are very happy about it … The site is marvellous … Not only are the mountains a pleasant sight, but … there is also beautiful Harrington Lake, about three miles long, where the fishing is very good and where splendid salmon, trout and big bass can still be got.

Still other properties are owned by the NCC and leased to permanent or summer residents. Both the Meech and Hope houses are leased, as is the Capucin Chapel. In addition, privately owned land still exists within the boundary of the Park, notably on Meech and Kingsmere lakes. Meanwhile, privately owned property on these two lakes continues to be subdivided, sold, and new homes built, all within park boundaries.

Talk about "carrying capacity." Somehow this seems to refer only to the public. What of the limits to private ownership in the park?

The jury is still out on whether or not private ownership is "right" within Gatineau Park — or any other park, for that matter. For now, an uneasy truce remains, possibly because the NCC cannot afford the going market value of privately held land.

COMPETING INTERESTS

The Kingsmere cottage area typifies the constant struggle between government and private interests. Private citizens living along Kingsmere, Barnes, and Swamp roads grumble about the streams of cars and tourists passing by their properties. As public access increases, park roads become worn and increasingly congested for cyclists and walkers. Yet townsfolk and tourists demand recreational outlets, and tourism is a burgeoning industry bringing undeniable prosperity to the National Capital Region.

The NCC and bordering municipalities try to balance these interests. But they too have historically had an uneasy peace. Each has their own mandates and jurisdictions. And the municipalities always resented the significant loss of revenue when their taxpayers (farmers, loggers, cottagers) were bought out by the FDC.

There are no easy answers. Gatineau Park was born out of a struggle lasting years. Now that it exists, environmental concerns continue to vie with equally contested private and public interests. Tragically, a quarter of a million dollars is spent each year fixing amenities that have been deliberately vandalized — facilities specifically erected for public use. It is no wonder that Gatineau Park staff often feel like scapegoats trapped in a no-win situation.

PUBLIC PARTICIPATION, PUBLIC PRESSURE

Today the NCC actively encourages the public's participation in information sessions. Master Plans, written every decade, undergo the scrutiny of public hearings where ordinary citizens determinedly voice their questions to Park planners and consultants. Why don't you allow us to rock climb on the Eardley Escarpment? Why don't you let us ride horseback in our park? Why won't you let us "harvest" deer and "edible animals" in our park? Why can't we ride our ATVs along the trails?

These questions imply the problem, I think: we consider the park our property. Is this right? Is it truly only our playground? What of the wildlife? And how much of "us" can the wildlife (plant or animal) actually tolerate?

In recognition of our demands, the NCC created some shared-use trails, such as Ridge Road (trail #1), and parts of the Trans-Canada Trail (see NCC ski or hiking trail maps) for example. Shared use demands an honour system of mutual respect. Mountain bikes and hikers are not necessarily incompatible users, but they can be if they are insensitive to one another's habits and needs. While snowmobilers were successfully banned from using their machines on trails in the "foot of the Park" near Pink and Fairy lakes in the 1960s, they continue to use trails in the supposed "wilderness sector" of Lac Philippe to the west. And in 1994, when Kennedy Road was suddenly claimed by skidooers, it was other park users who successfully lobbied to have them banned. The trail is now back to shared hiker/biker use in summer, and skiers in winter.

Other uses are being considered, tested, adopted, or rejected. Dog-sled circuits now exist and we have hut-to-hut skiing. But whatever the NCC decides, it's never the "right thing," it will never be "enough." Already, others complain that the distances between huts aren't challenging enough and that they don't meet international standards. NCC policy-makers and staff are caught between a rock and a hard place.

OUTREACH TO THE NEW MILLENNIUM

How will Gatineau Park survive as a healthy sanctuary for wildlife? How will it be able to satisfy the public's need to experience nature?

Park Director Jean René Doyon speaks of the continued, pressing need for education and interpretation. Otherwise, if the park acquiesces to all users' varied demands, we endanger those "cultural assets" (the historic homes, the fire tower, and the ruins, for example) as well as the ecosystems upon which the wild creatures depend. To preserve the park's varied habitats and assets, the NCC conducts environmental monitoring. Twenty percent of the trails are analyzed annually; thus every five years the entire circuit is done. Because of this, the impact of new user groups such as mountain bikers can be assessed. This will in turn, affect the shared trail system.

Doyon suggests the park needs a Visitor's Centre which would introduce people to the park and not simply tell people what they can and cannot do. We need to learn and understand the consequences of our actions. The Pink Lake restoration project of the 1980s is a superb example. Erosion of the lake's phosphorous-rich cliffs was killing the rare, meromitic lake; it was hikers, bikers, and swimmers who created the problem. The NCC closed the lake and, after a three-year restoration project including reforestation (by volunteer tree planters), interpretation, and the building of a boardwalk trail, access has been restored — and the lake saved.

As park users, we need to learn about cause and effect. We must understand how to protect that which we want to explore. Otherwise, more and more private homes will encroach upon our lakes and increasingly varied human desires will penetrate into the Lac Lapêche western sector, pushing the wildlife, like the two wolf packs, out of their park. Once outside the park, wolves can be shot. Is this really what we want our impact to be?

I believe in shared use between wildlife and human beings. In Gatineau Park, we are in their space. Do we have the courage to let the wild live and flourish in this brave new millennium? As Doyon says, we cannot expect to be able to hike, ski, bike and snowmobile "everywhere."

Really and truly: the future of our park lies beyond mere "legislation." Wisdom and responsible use is up to you and me.

PART TWO

Habitats to Discover

Are your senses at the ready? Are you prepared to listen for the scurrying rustle of movement in the undergrowth that hints of a white-footed mouse? Can you pause, take the time to listen to the songbirds trill their tunes and learn how to identify the singer? Are you ready to crouch down and peer silently into the pond life at your feet, to wonder at its teeming activity? Can you see the tadpole-so-soon-to-be-frog sporting odd-looking legs on its bulbous body? Can you recognize the season by its smell? Did you see the claw marks on the beech tree, telling you that a bear was by?

Either early spring or fall are by far the best times to experience such pleasures. After all, can you imagine sitting still — a target for the hosts of black flies, mosquitoes, deer and horse flies that are the bane of the summer hiker? Early spring and fall are also the most active for the wild creatures. In the spring, amid the rushing meltwater of swollen waterfalls, there is the serious business of finding a mate, of nest building and infant rearing in the protection of the shrubs, grasses, and woods. In midsummer's heat, when food is abundant, the woods adopt an atmosphere of waiting. The forest comes alive again in fall, with scurrying activity as creatures stock their winter larders. Let's not forget the season of snow, when you can "read" the tracks, discover the wing prints left by an owl as it swept a red squirrel from a snow bank. Frozen beaver ponds and lakes give us access to winter trails otherwise impassable: this is the magical season, when you can peer down a beaver's breathing hole in the ice, or follow a fox's tracks circling a muskrat lodge.

Before you start exploring the park, learn to listen and watch for the language of the wild. If the porcupine you've found starts to chatter, step back and don't alarm it further; respect the personal space of all the creatures. Remember: you are a visitor in their sanctuary.

Telltale clues that speak volumes about the beaver are easily spotted. Our national symbol is famous for its industrious felling of trees and dam building. Often the earliest hint that you're approaching a beaver pond is a grey stand of trees, their roots drowned, their tops dead. You may see totem poles of gnawed-off trees silently speaking of the time that a beaver chewed their trunks to create more logs for its dam. On the trail, search for a slick, still-wet swath of bent grasses and crushed undergrowth where a beaver struggled, pulling its burden of fresh-cut saplings down to the water's edge. On the muddy bank of the pond you might find the imprint of its paw.

Although beavers are more active in spring and fall — and more commonly seen at dawn and dusk — even on a summer's midday, it is well worth your time to find a comfortable perch by a pond's edge. Be silent and still: a perception of movement may reward you. Silently and darkly the beaver cuts the surface of the water, creating a V-formation of eddies and ripples that causes arrowhead and water lilies to bob in its wake. There, you moved: slap, splash goes his tail. As suddenly as it touched your consciousness, it disappears beneath the surface.

Beavers dramatically change the woodland habitat by selective logging practices: for example, they don't find conifers tasty. Sunlight floods onto the forest floor after the protective canopy has fallen and the increase in light and heat kills some undergrowth while nurturing the growth of other species. They also alter the water level, drowning the roots of maple and elm, while encouraging alders. Woodland ferns, grasses and flowers give way: reeds, arrowhead, water lily, marsh marigold, and blue flag iris take hold along damp pond edges.

The dams can be longer than a football field and higher than a tall person; I've seen one on Lac Lapêche well over 8 feet high. Dams create a still pond environment instead of a flowing stream. Insects such as the dragonfly and caddis fly, and amphibians like newts, toads, and frogs now find places to lay their eggs. Caddis fly larvae live in odd-looking "houses" they construct from leaves and twigs cemented together by their saliva. They attach themselves to waterweeds and grasses. Look carefully for spiky little larvae shells about as big as your thumbnail. Frogs lay their eggs in fluffy clusters, toads in long strings about the width of a pencil. Both are encased in a jelly-like substance. By peering into the edge of the pond in the spring, you will be able to spot the eggs.

Later on, in June, return to the pond and see the metamorphosis of eggs into tadpoles. They won't change into frogs for at least a year. Bullfrogs take a couple of years to become fully formed adults. You will be amazed at the thousands of tadpoles you see. It would seem that there must be millions of frogs produced, but lots of natural predators co-exist here.

Overhead, you may hear the rattling call of a belted kingfisher darting above the pond's surface, hunting. Look along floating logs or among the tufted islands of grass and iris to spy a painted or snapping turtle. Pause to scan the cattail-clad banks of the pond to see the statuesque form of a great blue heron. Carefully examine the mud around your feet: can you find tracks of a hungry raccoon? All these creatures will eagerly dine on hapless tadpoles. And so the checks and balances of the food chain create natural environmental controls.

On your walk you may see signs of beaver control structures aimed at deterring these resolute rodents from creating havoc with trails, boardwalks, and streams. Man-made wire fencing or diversion dams actually built in the water protect the mouths of culverts.

There are two significant positive aspects to beaver pond communities. First, beavers create diverse and rich habitats for plant and animal life that are uniquely different to a stream or open lake environment. For example, the greying skeletons of dead trees in beaver ponds provide nesting sites for such birds as the osprey, owl, and that social nester, the great blue heron. Heronries are fascinating places: I've seen upwards of fifty active nests in one. Second, beaver ponds provide useful reservoirs for fighting forest fires. However, the detrimental effects of beavers are numerous in a park setting. Floodwaters created by dams can irrevocably eliminate other equally precious ecosystems and rare species.

In Gatineau Park, the conflict between human beings and beavers is intensified due to the mixture of neighbouring private, municipal, and provincial roads and properties. Beavers "get in the way" of human needs and wants: washed-out roads, flooded properties and hiking trails, and felled trees conspire to threaten the rodent. The result is that beavers demand careful wildlife management.

Once a beaver deserts its pond to search for another environment, both the dam and lodge deteriorate. The ecosystem changes dramatically as the water level drops, and new life forms invade as drier conditions take over. The result is that a "beaver meadow" is created, attracting the white-tailed deer.

The meadows and open areas of Gatineau Park were primarily created by one of two agents, the beaver and man. Beaver ponds dry up and become "beaver meadows" in their transition from pond to grassland. Human beings continually impact the park: settlers cleared land for their homes and pastures; more recently, swaths were cut and are still maintained for hydro lines, cross-country and downhill skiing runs; and parkways, roads, and cottages were built. Such alterations in habitat offer their rewards to keen observers. Patience reveals a variety of creatures great and small living within these open spaces.

Dead trees in beaver meadows provide nesting sites for the great crested flycatcher, and tree swallows. Watch them fly unerringly into their tiny nest-holes, dragonflies clutched in their beaks. These trees provide important territorial landmarks from which many birds pause to survey, proclaim and defend their territories. Although we human beings like to believe that birds sing for the sheer joy of it, such factors as defence or mating rituals are far more likely catalysts. Be that as it may, on a glorious spring day, with the heat of the sun warming the earth, and a brilliant blue sky above you — well, don't you feel like singing?

Meadow grasses provide perches and nesting grounds for many Canadian songbirds. Here you'll find the bobolink, with its glossy black breast and gaily coloured gold-black-and-white back. Its call is a melodious, gurgling chuckle. Another grassland species is the robin-sized meadowlark. The male has a bright yellow breast with an unmistakable black "V" below its throat.

You will also find the American goldfinch here, a sparrow-sized bird. In summer the male's jet black wings provide brilliant contrast to his golden body. Goldfinches fly in a short bobbing flight pattern punctuated by cheerful-sounding twitters. Whereas the other two birds mentioned nest in the grasses, often at or close to ground level, the gold-finch nests in shrubs or trees sometimes as high as twenty feet above the ground. Because its diet is mainly composed of seeds, the goldfinch only begins nesting in midsummer, when food is in plentiful supply.

Watch for piles of lichen-covered rocks in park meadows, painstakingly dug from the soil by early settlers, who grew hay, potatoes, and raised cattle "up the mountain." Among these rock piles see if you can find a nest of garter snakes, basking in the heat of the sun.

Meadowland plants are widely varied depending upon factors such as how long the meadow has been in existence and whether it was

Swallowtail butterfly on honeysuckle, a non-native plant introduced
for landscaping. Champlain Lookout.
Photo: Katharine Fletcher, 1987.

cultivated. As you wander in these former pastures, look for the
introduced and wildly successful honeysuckle, cultivars like the bearded
iris, periwinkle, and even daffodils, hyacinth, and tulips. Their presence
is a clue that you are near an abandoned homestead site. They compete
with the native wild raspberry, wild rose, strawberry, orange hawkweed,
and black-eyed susan.

Don't be afraid to get "up-close and personal" with blooming
honeysuckle (or lilac) bushes. In full summer they come alive with
honeybees and butterflies, intent on getting the blossom's nectar. Find
monarchs, swallowtails, and viceroys crowding these bushes, so absorbed
in their purpose that they will allow you an opportunity for prolonged
observation and photography — if you are still. The swallowtail's long,
slender "tongue" is amazing to see as it curls its way into the narrow
throat of the flowers. Look too for the hawk-moth, often mistaken for
tiny hummingbirds.

The verge between pasture and wood, or cleared edges on trails
like Ridge Road, is particularly rich with habitats, being the boundary

zones that attract the widest variety of wildlife. The McCloskey meadow (see McCloskey walk), for example, is an ideal location to look and listen for American redstarts, orioles, vireos, and perhaps my favourite of all, indigo buntings. The male is a deep blue-black colour that reflects the light so that, if you catch him in the sunlight, he can appear to be a brilliant neon blue. You will soon learn to recognize this lovely bird's trilling warble, a cheerful song to the open air.

White-tailed deer love the grasses of the beaver meadows and marshes, and can be best spotted either here or along the edge of open grassland. As you explore through spring to fall, note the change in their appearance: in early spring they have a gaunt look after surviving a rigorous Canadian winter. By early summer the coat has changed from grey-brown to the red-chestnut colour we normally associate with them. From now 'til late fall they eat heartily, first to feed their fawns and secondly, to put on the fat required to get them through the coming snows. Favourite foods include young saplings like beech. Cedars are real temptations for deer, just as appealing as chocolate to some of us. At such places as Blanchet Beach, look at the far side of Meech Lake. Can you see that the bottom of the cedars rimming the water's edge look as trimmed as some people's garden hedges? Deer stand on their hind legs on the frozen lake in winter, stretching up as high as they can reach to nibble the delectable greens.

At the verges be alert and ever-ready in June for the rare view of a fawn curled up in the summer sunshine. They are not at all easy to see, being cleverly camouflaged in their chestnut coats dappled with white spots. They blend in with the earth tones of the ground on which they nestle. The doe leaves her well-hidden baby in the tall grass while she forages for food: up to fifteen pounds of twigs, grasses, and leaves daily. Since newborn fawns have little scent for their first week after birth, the doe leaves them so that her odour will not attract predators. Mind you, she does not desert them: she returns for regular feedings and keeps a watchful eye on her tiny charges.

However tempting, do not touch a fawn; as with all wild things, leave them alone. Babies of any species are especially tempting for children, who want to pet bunnies or fawns. This is a good opportunity for you to teach young ones the lifelong lesson of looking, not touching. Explain to children that wild mothers may abandon young that have been touched, or a nest that has been poked.

After observing the life of the open meadow, you may be ready to plunge into the dappled shade of the woods. In early spring, there are especially tantalizing sounds beckoning us: the gurgling of brooks cascading down impromptu waterfalls, the last large-crystalled "corn" snow crunching beneath your feet. Buds swell to bursting capacity and the entire forest floor surges with life ready to unfold. In the trees, birds such as the rose-breasted grosbeak and scarlet tanager sing their songs.

Painted Trillium. Photo: Katharine Fletcher, 1990.

Up come the trilliums, their nodding heads forming a spring carpet of white, crimson, and pink. The less-common painted trillium grows by Lusk Cave, and Meech and Black lakes, as do our graceful representatives of the orchid family, the showy (pink and white) lady's slipper and the yellow lady's slipper. Here, too, you will find the orange wood lily, its characteristic trumpet face pointing skywards, stretching towards the sunshine. Down by your feet creeps the delicate twinflower, freshly scented wintergreen and myriads of blue, lavender, white, and yellow violets. Also in spring, look for the stately jack-in-the-pulpit in wet ground. Like the bunchberry, Solomon's seal, and clintonia, this member of the lily family is equally dramatic in the fall, brightening up the forest floor with its brilliant scarlet berries.

When you can, take some extra time to appreciate the woods. Find a likely looking spot and sit down. Make yourself comfortable, close your eyes, and concentrate on becoming a sensory receiver. Can you smell the forest floor? Can you detect the scent of humus, the dark, wet smell of a stream, the heady smell of pine, or the gassy smell of a nearby swamp? Can you hear the teasing "chuk, chuk" of a red squirrel warning woodland dwellers of your presence? Do you hear the scampering of a chipmunk building its nest in the dry leaves? Give yourself a chance to feel the textures of the woods. Let your hands wander over the ground where you sit, and touch the lichen clinging to a rock or the sharpness of a pine needle. Feel the warmth of sunshine touch your cheek and just as fleetingly leave you cool, as a cloud passes by overhead. Permit yourself this luxury of being at one with the woods.

Young groundhog at Taylor Lake. Photo: Katharine Fletcher, 1987.

During spring, see how many nests you can spot. Can you identify their owners? Compare the nest of the American redstart to the beautiful basketry of the Baltimore oriole. Observe what materials are used and contrast them to the nests of birds that dwell in marshes and meadows. Some birds such as the robin and the hooded warbler build their nests surprisingly close to the ground. I once found a robin's nest on top of a half-metre high stump. Its sky-blue eggs were gone within a week, perhaps making a tasty snack for a fox or raccoon.

Notice how sounds become distorted in the woods. The rustle of a chipmunk can sound like something ten times its size, while the white-tailed deer can be soundless. There is many a time I've heard the rat-a-tat-tat of what I took to be a woodpecker drilling a tree, only to be confounded by finding yet another small downy woodpecker as its source, instead of the anticipated large pileated woodpecker. Noise bounces off trunks and rocks, which magnify and distort the sounds. Perhaps not a small part of the distortion is psychological. There's a delicious spine-tingling sensation that comes over you when you're absolutely sure a bear is just around the corner …

Black bears are not uncommon in Gatineau Park. And sometimes, as in 1995, populations explode. During that year, food supplies were scant throughout the region and there were many forest fires to the north. Bears were hungry and looking for food "everywhere": in the park, and even wandering into downtown Hull and Ottawa. My husband Eric, on a hike with his English cousins in the park's western sector north of Quyon, was surrounded by eight adults plus their cubs. Their almost-unheard-of encounter was captured on video. For all that, park staff still tell me there have been no reported incidents of bears attacking anyone. Let's keep this record.

Learn to identify trees. The American beech has silver-grey, smooth bark that may have permanent claw marks wounding its trunk. Bears consider beech nuts a delicacy and clamber up the tree trunk to the canopy of the beech tree to eat them. The beech's smooth bark provides an especially good, permanent record of the bear's imprint. In fact, while the bear is dining at the top of the tree, it does a lot of damage, breaking boughs as it reaches out and "rakes" the nuts toward its jaws, with its strong paws and claws. Get a close-up view of the claw marks, *but first check that that bruin isn't still aloft.*

White-tailed deer on gravel spit at Lac Philippe.
Photo: Laurie Schell, 1987.

People constantly ask me about bears — especially after they see their claw marks in beech trees. Remember: back off and never be aggressive if you see one. Never feed bears and don't advance towards them with your camera at the ready. Promote wildlife wisdom by setting a good example to your friends and kids alike: wild animals are unpredictable. Our wild bruins just don't possess Winnie-the-Pooh's amicable nature.

The slow-moving porcupine is among the other creatures that leave their claw marks on bark. You can detect the damage they leave, notably on wild cherry trees and poplars, which they consider delicious. (This habit does not endear them either to woodlot owners or park staff.) Watch for the porcupine's smaller claw marks on the smooth bark of young poplars. You may even find a quill or two embedded in the bark. Look up at the canopy: often you can spot a "porky" munching away happily, well out of harm's way. Porcupines have a special weakness for salt, which prompts me to advise: do not be dismayed to find a porcupine in the outhouses scattered about Gatineau Park. Salt, which is in our urine and exudes from perspiration on our hands as we grasp door handles, is like a magnet to them. Park staff wage a constant battle with porcupines, regularly replacing door handles, toilet seats, and even table-tops at the lodges.

As for shooting their quills — they don't. But avoid provoking the peace-loving porcupine. If you see one on the forest floor, watch it from a distance. Note its slow, waddling gait. If you approach too closely, you may see it halt and hear its "ch-ch-ch" sound of warning, plainly telling you to keep your distance. You may also see the quills rising on its back, see the skin rippling and tail start to swing back and forth. If you do, back off, for you may quite literally be too close for comfort. Quills are loosely attached to the porcupine's skin and some will come off with the motion of the tail. However, they do not loosely attach themselves to your skin: they become embedded immediately. They are excruciating to remove because of nasty barbs along the shaft at the tip. And, if you happen to be in the park with your dog (which of course is on a leash) pull your animal back.

THE EARDLEY ESCARPMENT

For a completely different environment atypical to this area, explore the Eardley Escarpment, the ridge of high land forming the southern boundary of Gatineau Park. (See Champlain, Wolf, King Mountain, and Luskville Falls walks: all give you close-up introductions to this fascinating microclimate.)

Because of its extreme southerly aspect, the ridge receives more warm sunlight than any other area of the park. You only have to sit on its Precambrian rock, revelling in the view of the Ottawa Valley, to fully appreciate its hot, dry habitat. Different species of plants that are especially adapted to these conditions are found here, such as the eastern red cedar, a member of the juniper family more commonly found in southern Ontario. This tree likes well drained, rocky ridges. Here on the ridge, the degree of exposure to the elements combined with lack of moisture stunts the trees. The red oak is similarly adapted, being stunted and compact.

Take binoculars if you're headed to the ridge. If you are lucky, you will be treated to spectacular gliding shows of the red-tailed hawk or turkey vulture which soar on the updrafts of wind along the escarpment edge. Listen for the red-tailed hawk's elemental cry of the wild on the wind. Peer at the vulture with its blood-red, naked head and marvel at its wingspan. Unlike the hawk, this scavenger often searches for carrion in groups of as many as a dozen, always in silence.

Keep a lookout for eagles, particularly along the western, more remote sector of the escarpment face. From the Eardley Road west to the Steele Line, look for golden and bald eagles. Not far from here, in the winter of 2002, a hawk owl was spied, a rare visitor to this region.

Along the escarpment face, you discover grasses and sedges, important additions to the environment because they keep the shallow topsoil from blowing or washing away. If you're unsure of the difference between sedges and grasses, bend down to feel the stem. Sedge has a definite three-sided, triangular shape distinguishing it from grass. Look for the other shrubs and plants which assist the grasses at their task. You will see the wild rose casting its perfume into the still heat of a summer's day. Columbines abound, their jaunty red jester caps having bright yellow tips on their spurs.

In winter, the escarpment gets less snow coverage than the northern stretches of the park. In the very late fall, prior to the first snowfall, white-tailed deer head for the steeply sloped area which provides easier foraging and protection from the cold and from predators.

These are just a few profiles of some significant habitats to discover in Gatineau Park. You will find many others, such as bogs, which offer endless opportunity for discovery and excitement.

Listen, watch for, and respect the language of wildlife. Stay back: respect the personal space of all the creatures with whom we share our world. Finally, please don't remove species from the park: maintain their sanctuary.

PART THREE

Trails that Beckon

First Things First: Getting to Gatineau Park

How do you get to Gatineau Park? Several ways depending on what trails you choose. Examine the map at the back of this guide, which shows all trails described in this book. Which part of the park are you going to? Is it your first visit? If so, I strongly recommend you check out the Visitor's Centre in Old Chelsea, so you can familiarize yourself with the park, with NCC services, and with other routes into Gatineau Park. If you are new to the park, why not make your first excursion the Sugar Bush Loop? It is particularly appropriate because it is open year-round as a walking trail.

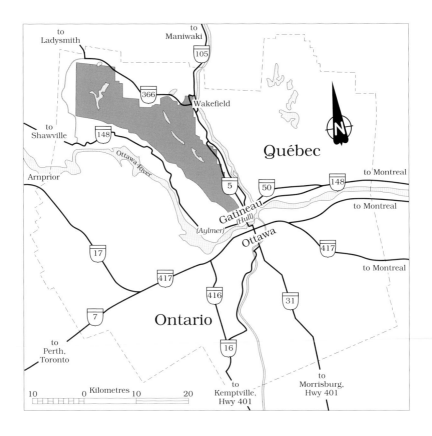

One visitor reception area lies north of Gamelin Boulevard in Gatineau (formerly Hull). To find it, drive north on the Gatineau Parkway (the entrance is on Alexandre Taché Boulevard, opposite Harvey's restaurant); after 1 km you arrive at the Gamelin Visitor Kiosk where you can find maps, books, and information from park staff. There is also an excellent introductory trail, the Pioneer Trail, located just west of the parking lot. It forms a simple loop and introduces you to some of the tree species in the park, as well as training your eyes to look for clues of human habitation. (Note the metre stick attached to a sign at this trail's entrance, which handily measures snow depth. This well-interpreted trail is maintained as a walking path in winter.)

The main Visitor's Centre is in the village of Old Chelsea, a fifteen-minute drive from Parliament Hill. Head north through Hull on Highway 5. Take the Old Chelsea exit at the NCC Gatineau Park sign, carefully turn left and then cross the overpass into the village. Watch for Scott Road and turn right. The park headquarters are the first left. Here you'll find the Visitor's Centre. **Note:** the old Visitor's Centre, located off Meech Lake Road west of Old Chelsea, was closed in 1999. The building, Harrison House, still stands alongside Sugar Bush trail. Its future remains uncertain. Like many buildings designed as private homes, its design poses challenges for re-use.

VISITOR'S CENTRE

Visitor's Centre staff will help you orient yourself to the park and decide which trails best suit you. Gatineau Park offers many options: from paved walks for handicapped access to challenging hill hikes, bike routes, and ski circuits. As well, several trails interconnect from Wakefield southeast past Old Chelsea and Pink Lake to Gatineau (formerly Hull) as a part of the Trans-Canada Trail system. You will find tranquil lakes for canoeing, overnight summer and winter camping facilities, and huts you can book, for a fee, for yourself or a group. Staff is updated twice daily on weather and winter ski conditions, and emergency communication systems at all of the park's eight lodges connect you with the centre, should you require emergency help. The Visitor Centre phone number is 819-827-2020 (or toll-free 1-800-827-2020). It is located at 33 Scott Road, Old Chelsea, Quebec (open 7 days a week from 9:00h to 17:00h. Information is also available from the Capital Infocentre in Ottawa at 90 Wellington Street (613-230-5000 or 1-800-465-1865, open 7 days a week from 9:00h to 17:00h). Mailing address is Gatineau Park, National Capital Commission, 202-40 Elgin Street, Ottawa, Ontario, Canada K1P 1C7; e-mail: gpvisito@ncc-ccn.ca; Internet: www.capcan.ca

WHAT ELSE DOES THE VISITOR'S CENTRE OFFER?

- It has a superb relief map showing the topography of Gatineau Park: the elevation of the ridge; the faulted channel of Philippe, Harrington, and Meech lakes; and the pastureland of the Meech Creek Valley.

- It sells summer and winter trail maps that are useful companions to this guide.

- Ask about the trail numbering and colour system. Numbers identify trails; colours identify degree of difficulty, primarily for skiing but they give you an idea of difficulty for walking and biking, too (green = easy; blue = intermediate; red with black diamond = difficult).

- Learn about trail access: familiarize yourself well with the shared trail network. Bicycles are not allowed on all summer trails and the bike season is limited to May through October (ask for the season's dates). In winter, you can snowshoe anywhere "off-trail" in the park — but not on all trails, nor can you walk on all trails in winter. Because the shared trails system may change, please check for up-to-the-minute rules on which trail can be used for what purpose.

- Parkways are closed to traffic in winter after the first snowfall, opening late April or early May, after danger of ice is past.

- User fees apply to beach parking lots in summer and to winter trails. You can purchase a season's or a daily pass at the centre. There is an honour system of money boxes and tags at the trailheads, and trails are patrolled.

- A maximum of two dogs per person is allowed and these must be on leashes. No dogs are allowed on beaches. Check with the Visitor Centre staff for current information.

- In-line skaters use the parkway system throughout the spring/summer/fall season. When driving, use extreme caution: unfortunately, the skaters sometimes weave five-deep over the road and represent an "accident waiting to happen."

THE TRAILS

I have described twenty-four walks that incorporate many significant historical sites. As of 2004, in summer the NCC maintain more than 90 km of shared hiking and biking trails, and more than 75 km of paths devoted only to hiking. In winter, there are 200 km of groomed ski trails. The trail network includes 35 km of Trans-Canada Trail, which connect to the National Capital Region's recreational pathway. Check with the Visitor's Centre for the current status of the shared trail network because the type of use fluctuates: for example, a few trails are kept open solely for winter walking and snow shoeing.

LONGER EXCURSIONS: CAMPING AND HUT-TO-HUT

Overnight camping is available at Philippe, Taylor, and La Pêche lakes. You can book Brown Lake cabin for an overnight stay. Call the Visitor's Centre to make your reservations.

BEFORE YOU GO: SOME TIPS

- During summer the Park's roads are closed on Sunday mornings from May until the end of September. This allows cyclists, in-line skaters, and hikers to fully enjoy and explore the parkway network.
- Gatineau Park is "wild." Be aware that you can be fairly remote very soon.
- Stay on designated trails. Remember this is a wildlife sanctuary for animals, birds, fish, and plants. This is their home territory and, after all, it's nature that we want to appreciate.
- Plan your outing and tell someone where you are going, your destination, and estimated return time.
- Footwear is crucial: wear comfortable, flat-soled, sturdy shoes — not a new pair.
- Take a daypack (ensure the zippers are sound) so that your hands are free to use the binoculars and camera around your neck. (For longer hikes, consider a first-aid kit.)
- In bug season (mid-May through the end of July), take insect repellent.

- Pack a lunch and trail treats.
- Always take extra drinks: water is best.
- Take identification books for flowers, animals, birds, rocks.
- Learn to identify and avoid poison ivy.
- Be smart about clothing: layering is best; wool keeps you warm even if wet; microfibre, as in "river pants" is both wind and water resistant and if soaked it dries easily. Wear a hat for warmth, to discourage bugs, to protect you from rain, sleet, or snow, and to shield you from the sun.
- Leave nothing but your footprints on the trail.
- Dog note: NCC regulations stipulate that dogs must be kept on a leash no more than 2 metres long. A maximum of two dogs per person is permitted. Dogs may only use official summer trails; they are not allowed on Pink, King Mountain, or Luskville Falls trails. Rules change: to be sure, check with the Visitor's Centre.

PRELIMINARY NOTES TO THE TRAIL DESCRIPTIONS

- Find the legend for the trail maps and a general access map to Gatineau Park at the back of the book.
- *Historical Walks* is primarily a hiking guide. If you want to bike, confirm which trails are shared because a significant number are not open to bicyclists. Call Camp Fortune to find out more about their 12 km of biking trails (819-827-1717 or 1-888-283-1717 toll free). Skiers will soon realize that winter's snow gives access to lakes and routes that are naturally barred from summer access by water, beaver dams, or other natural phenomena. Enquire at the Visitors' Centre for information on winter trails, some are maintained for cross-country, others for snowshoe or walking trails. There are two types of ski trails: Some are track groomed for classic style skiing; others are groomed flat and wide for ski-skating. There is also a training circuit for those of you who wish to do cross-country ski marathons. Also, a section of Wolf Trail is a designated snowshoe trail. Some trails are compacted in winter for walking (such as Lauriault and Sugar Bush). Because trail usage and maintenance fluctuates with varying demand, always check with the Visitors' Centre to see which trails are used for what purpose.

- Hikes are identified by an alphabetic character (A–X). Each is listed on the map at the back of the book.

- Each hike description gives directions to the Park from Ottawa. If you approach from a different orientation, refer to the map at the back of the book.

- All distances and times are approximate. One trail may be shorter than another in distance, but the timing longer if it is more difficult or if there are many things to do and see.

- "Trailhead" means the start of a trail.

- Abbreviations: NCC = National Capital Commission; P-7, P-11 represent parking lot numbers, but not all lots are numbered; TCT = Trans-Canada Trail.

- For trails, wherever possible, I have used the old names originally selected by the Trail and Night Riders of the Ottawa Ski Club. However, I have also included the numbering system used on the NCC maps.

- **Important:** If you see something amiss on the trail, such as a fallen tree or a flooded spot, report it to the NCC Visitor's Centre.

- Finally, have fun: enjoy and preserve Gatineau Park.

The sugar shack in winter, photographed at its original location along the Sugar Bush trail. It is now located near the Visitor's Centre marking the start of this trail. Photo: Katharine Fletcher, 1997.

A: SUGAR BUSH LOOP

4-season hiking/winter walking
1.5 km return
Allow 40 minutes

This leisurely amble gives a good introduction to the Park, located just behind the Old Chelsea Visitor's Centre at 33 Scott Road, Old Chelsea.

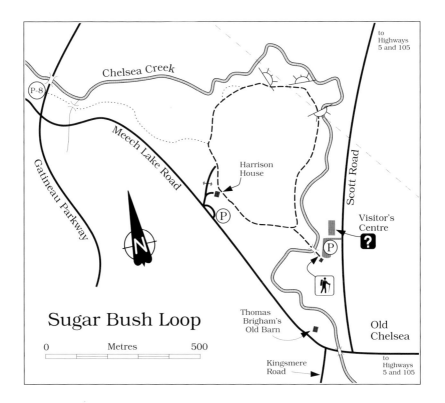

Access: The Old Chelsea Visitor's Centre is a fifteen minute drive from Parliament Hill. Head north through Hull on Highway 5. Take the Old Chelsea exit after the NCC Gatineau Park sign. Carefully turn left and cross the overpass into the village. Turn right on Scott Road: your first left is the Visitor's Centre, park museum, and park administration buildings. Park here.

Facilities: Informative staff at the Visitor's Centre can answer your questions about the park. You'll find washrooms, picnic tables here. As well, there is snowshoe rental in winter. Also you can find out about the Friends of Gatineau Park here. **Note:** The old Visitor's Centre used to be 0.5 km west on the Meech Lake Road. At time of writing, it is being considered for the site of the Canadian Ski Museum but this is not official. Enquire at the Visitor's Centre.

Trail description: The trailhead is at the western edge of the parking lot, beside the cabin. It is a short stroll down to the bridge spanning the Chelsea Creek. As you cross it, look down to search for paw prints in the sandy embankments below you. Can you find raccoon prints? You're soon over the creek: turn right when you reach the main path, which runs along the wending banks of the creek, eventually going through some hemlock trees.

The trail reaches a pine plantation where it veers left. For another view of the now-widening watercourse, head right past a large white pine. Hydro poles span the creek and march up the opposite hillside.

Return to the trail, heading right. The main path narrows and stays left. You soon see another path near some hemlocks, heading right to the creek again. Go this way for a spectacular view up the now-wide creek bed to the ridge. In winter you can see the gondola lifts of Camp Fortune heading up the ski runs. Before you retrace your steps to the main path, look around you: can you see the old fence posts?

Head right at the main trail. Now you will veer right, ignoring the path that heads left. Pass a bench on your right and, just beyond and behind it, take another detour right. From this vantage point, you can look back at the lookout you just visited.

Return to the main path. The trail forks here: why not head up along the narrower path on your right? You go up and down along this hilly trail, eventually reaching a large rocky outcrop with a cave-like base, full of water. Take care: watch your footing. Now descend through mixed hardwoods (lots of mature black cherry trees here) to the main path. A sign points 700 metres, right, to P-8 at the intersection of the Gatineau Parkway. Continue left, to walk 200 metres past the old Park Visitor's Centre via a second "overflow" gravel parking lot in the woods (now closed to the public). Continue on the broad trail, the former visitor's centre (Harrison House) on your right. A meadow appears on your right, directly after the building. Proceed straight and soon you come to the junction with the path over the bridge, the start of your walk. Ahead of you is the old sugar shack, the Visitor's Centre on Scott Road, and your car.

Intersecting trails: As noted, there is an unnumbered trail connecting Sugar Bush to Chelsea parking lot, P-8, which is at the junction of Meech Lake Road and Gatineau Parkway. Notably in winter, when you can snowshoe along the Gatineau Parkway, this trail makes a more challenging route.

Points of interest: Chelsea Creek used to be known as Brook's Creek after a settler of that name. The creek's falls (between Scott and Kingsmere roads) once boasted Thomas Brigham's saw and gristmills, which were built by Josiah Chamberlin. Even further downstream was Seldon Church's tannery. Despite the fact there are no ruins or remnants left to see, this walk introduces us to the importance of water courses to settlements.

The Sugar Bush Loop is also important as a reminder of how early settlers quickly learned how to make maple sugar and syrup. The NCC built the sugar shack you see here in 1972, operating it for several winters until cutbacks forced its closure. Today it offers welcome shelter at the start or end of your walk.

B: OLD CHELSEA CEMETERY

Historic site
700 metres
Allow 30 minutes

The Old Chelsea Protestant Cemetery is a quiet graveyard situated in a clearing beside Chelsea Creek. Here find the grave of Asa Meech, after whom Meech Lake was named.

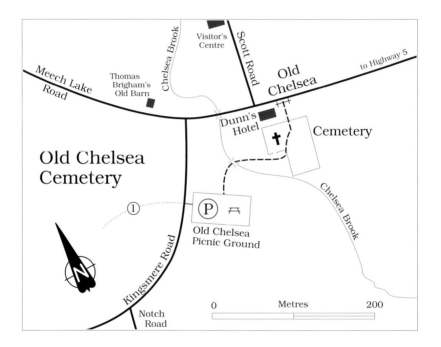

Access: Turn left to Old Chelsea from Highway #5. About 500 metres past Scott Road, take the left-hand turn onto Kingsmere Road. Almost immediately to your left is the Old Chelsea Picnic Ground parking lot. Park here.

Facilities: At the parking lot there are toilets, picnic tables, and barbecue pits.

Trail description: The trailhead is on the north side of the parking lot. Descend the stairway leading to a bridge over Chelsea Creek. Turn to your right after crossing the creek and head up the incline to the clearing in the woods. This is the cemetery. During the summer, the gravestones nestle amid purple-flowering, fragrant wild thyme. **Note:** I've suggested viewing a few other sites of interest, found along Meech Lake Road in the village of Old Chelsea. If you wish, exit the cemetery through its ornate gates to explore the village, then retrace your steps to your car.

Intersecting trails: None.

Points of interest: Today, Chelsea Creek appears extremely diminutive, albeit pretty. As you gaze left while standing on the wooden bridge spanning the ravine, it is difficult to imagine that this watercourse once was a prosperous industrial site. Prior to the rerouting of the Meech Lake/Old Chelsea Road, remnants of Thomas Brigham's 1822 saw and gristmills existed on either side of the brook below the Kingsmere Road overpass.

Consecrated as the Old Chelsea Protestant Cemetery in 1891, this is one of the oldest cemeteries in the area. You will discover it directly behind the tin-covered former Dunn's Hotel. Asa Meech and his wife Margaret Docksteader Meech are buried here, as are approximately fifty other early settlers. Here you'll find the graves of the Alexander family who owned and operated Meech Lake House in 1914, and Thomas Wright is also laid to rest here, a son of Philemon. Thomas' 1801 gravestone represents one of the earliest marked graves in the National Capital Region. The cemetery is L-shaped; continue to its easternmost end then turn right: you'll find more gravestones overlooking the creek.

The original wrought iron gates leading to the cemetery were probably the handiwork of the blacksmith, Philip Leppard whose shop was one of many thriving businesses in Old Chelsea years ago. Leppard's shop was just east of here, near St. Stephen's Church parking lot. Another business was the tannery, located beside the brook at the end of a little lane that joined the village road opposite today's Chelsea Restaurant (the former 1824 Dean's Hotel). If you explore Chelsea Creek downstream of the cemetery you may find a few stone ruins, all that is left of Seldon Church's tannery. Hemlocks are found here: the bark of these trees was used in the tanning process.

Asa Meech's gravestone at the Old Protestant Burying Grounds,
Old Chelsea. Photo: Katharine Fletcher, September 2002.

When you cross Chelsea Creek, imagine what industry used to be
connected with waterways in the not-too-distant past. Look left to the
falls: by 1822 Thomas Brigham operated both a sawmill and gristmill
here. (Brigham's barn remains standing in its original spot, opposite
the Kingsmere Road turnoff on the other side of Meech Lake Road.)
His homestead, now called the Brigham-Chamberlin House due to
intermarriage of the two settler families, is the oldest house in the
village. Originally located near the barn beside the creek, it was moved
in 1962 to its present location on Padden Road.

As an intriguing contrast, consider walking east on Old Chelsea
Road to visit St. Stephen's Roman Catholic Church completed in
1882. Construction of it began in 1879 from leftover stones cut from
the Corkstown quarry, near Kanata. (Stone from this quarry was also
used for the parliament buildings.) Imagine how long it took to haul
the stone by horse and wagon ... Men and their teams of horses left
the village near dawn with goods to be sold at Byward market in
Ottawa, then they would continue to Parliament Hill where they'd
load their wagons with stones. The trek back would see them home by
10:00 p.m. or so.

C: MEECH LAKE 1 — THE RUINS

Shared bike/hike/ski trail: #36, TCT & unnumbered path
3.25 km return
Allow 2 hours for the ruins

Walk through a predominantly hardwood forest to find the ruins of Thomas "Carbide" Willson's fertilizer plant. Only part of this trail is a shared trail (#36).

Please note: Although discouraged by the NCC, these ruins are the favourite retreat of nude sunbathers. If your sensibilities will be offended, by all means avoid this area; otherwise feel free to go and enjoy the walk as you would any other. An early morning start (6:00 a.m. or so) may permit you to wander around the ruins freely — and to get your photos before the appearance of a camera causes any misunderstandings. Otherwise, walk during bug season (mid-May through July) when nudists take cover.

"Carbide" Willson's acid condensation tower, dam, footbridge, and generating station, July 13, 1917. The falls are the start of Meech Creek, below which there was quite a "village" community. Photo by Topley. NAC PA–144964.

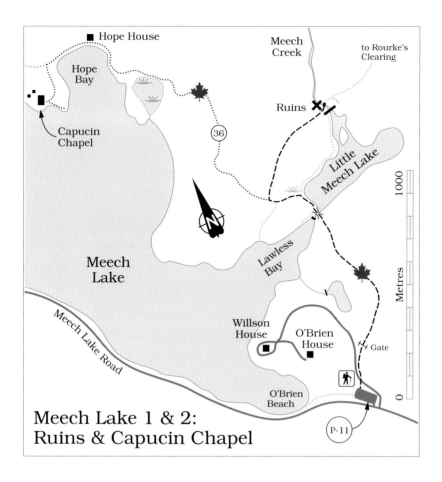

Meech Lake 1 & 2:
Ruins & Capucin Chapel

Access: The most direct route is to take the Meech Lake Road from Old Chelsea and continue to O'Brien Beach P-11 on your right. Or, take the Champlain Parkway, and turn right on Fortune Lake Parkway. Turn right and continue to the Meech Lake Road; now turn left, continuing to O'Brien Beach. **Note:** In season when the beaches are open, there is a fee for parking.

Facilities: Outhouses at O'Brien Beach; changing facilities and garbage bins at the parking lot. **Tips:** On summer weekends the lot is often full. You can canoe on Meech Lake, be wary: it's a big, long lake so winds blow up quickly, creating whitecaps. A brief lift of a portage gets you into Little Meech Lake.

Trail description: Start at the northwest corner of P-11, at the gravel road. This restricted access road is NCC-maintained and RCMP-patrolled; both the O'Brien and Willson homes are government retreats and barred from public use.

Proceed on foot up the road until you reach the well-worn Trans-Canada Trail (formerly the Discovery trail) #36 heading off to your right (north) through the woods: a distance of about .25 km. (If you come to the stone pillars and iron gate marking the entrance to the Willson estate, turn back, for you've gone too far.)

Head along the footpath; your keen eye will spot the NCC sign declaring that nudism is illegal here. It's surely worth a photograph ... Continue over gentle hills for about 700 metres and you soon come to a wide, steep descent to a sturdy bridge spanning a watercourse, the outflow of Meech into Little Meech Lake. While descending, look for the small holes in the embankment: this is a veritable "chipmunk condo." Imagine them scurrying along, sheltered by the mossy overhangs. As you cross the bridge, Meech Lake is on your left; Little Meech to your right. Look for merganser ducks and loons, or listen for the rattling laugh of the kingfisher.

Thomas "Carbide" Willson's dam, Meech Lake, July 13, 1917. Note extent of clearing behind dam, complete with shacks and possibly a potato patch on the right. Photo by Topley. NAC PA–144967.

At the end of the bridge, veer right to follow the shoreline for 100 metres. There is a fork in the trail at the end of the bay. Stay left, up a short, fairly steep incline for approximately 100 metres. Pass the broad trail leading down to Lawless Bay, staying on your trail for another 50 metres until you reach another well-worn path to the right. Head right, and continue uphill for .5 km to the ruins. Cross the headwaters of Meech Creek. In winter, this picturesque waterfall has that lovely blue ice. In the early days, logs were floated down the creek to Cascades, on the Gatineau River.

Return to your car by retracing your steps.

Intersecting trails: A honeycomb of trails is found here; stay on the main path.

Points of interest: By 1904, Thomas "Carbide" Willson had purchased 400 acres at Meech Lake where he built his summer residence, completed three years later. The ruins of the generating station and acid condensation tower form the destination of this hike. The super-phosphate fertilizer plant was the first of its kind in the world. Patrick Farrell had already built a dam at the headwaters of Meech Creek for his sawmill and Willson adapted it to his needs.

Today, the electrical generating plant stands bereft of windows and roof. In fact, its iron beams and galvanized roofing was recovered during the Depression. The penstock, which funnelled water into the station's turbines, is all but gone: you can see where it once lay, and can appreciate why the NCC has fenced off its mouth. On the opposite side of Meech Creek, only the base of the acid condensation tower remains, the rest was destroyed by fire.

Willson's home, along with its 1930s neighbour, the J. Ambrose O'Brien home (known as Kinora Lodge), are both at the southeast end of Meech Lake. The NCC purchased Kinora Lodge in 1979. That year they also acquired the Willson property and designated it a heritage building. Unfortunately the picturesque O'Brien house next door is rapidly deteriorating; hopefully it will be restored to its former architectural splendour. Although the Department of Public Works operates the Willson residence as a government conference centre, O'Brien house has been seriously neglected. The NCC has solicited private-sector proposals for its use variously as an inn, training, or other type of centre but to date, the old residence stands forlorn and unused.

D: MEECH LAKE 2 — CAPUCIN CHAPEL

Hike/ski trail: #36
& unmarked hike-only loop
5.5 km return
Allow 2 hours

This hilly walk affords picturesque views of Meech Lake and the "back" of the Eardley Escarpment ridge. Because it takes you near private cottages, please respect residents' privacy and grounds.

Access: (See Meech Lake 1 walk.)

Facilities: (See Meech Lake 1 walk.)

Trail description: *(Refer to map on page 100:* The trail to the Capucin Chapel appears as a dotted line on the map, so as not to be confused with Meech Lake 1: Ruins walk.) Follow exactly the same instructions for that walk until you reach the right-hand trail to the ruins.

Instead of turning right, stay on the main path. Continue for about 1 km, going up and down relatively hilly (albeit gentle) terrain. You pass a large wetland on your left, formerly a beaver pond where many drowned trees make excellent nesting sites for birds. Continue on the path; as you loop around the old pond you suddenly are in a tiny grove of pine and, on a hot summer's day, their fragrance is heady. At your feet here, find wintergreen. In spring, the hill on the left is full of bellwort, trilliums, spring beauties, hepaticas, and Dutchman's breeches. Turn a corner and there is Meech Lake. The path now hugs the shoreline alongside striped (white) gentians, boneset, and Joe-Pye-Weed growing in the sandy soil. There is a lot of beaver activity here: constantly renovated lodges in Hope Bay and trails through the grasses leading to the water's edge. Ahead of you now is the boathouse and Hope House, former home of John Hope. In early summer, see butterflies and ruby-throated hummingbirds hovering over the lilac blossoms here.

Continue past the boathouse. Meech Lake is directly on your left. Just as your trail starts to rise through the woods, at the very end of the lake, look for a very narrow path going left. It hugs the bay, leading you beside cedar trees. Avoid this trail because it is becoming severely eroded. Head up the wide main trail that ascends a short rise. Look for a pathway veering left through the woods and walk down it. Soon you can glimpse Meech Lake and the Capucin Chapel ahead of you. (See the map on page 100.) Return to O'Brien, P-11 by retracing your steps.

Hope House on Hope Bay, Meech Lake, after its renovation of 1962.
NCC historical file #05–0081000–00163.

Intersecting trails: No major trail intersections. (Trail #36 continues to connect with #50, which will take you to Herridge Lodge and Lac Philippe.)

Points of interest: In 1900 the Capucin Friars of L'Église St. François d'Assissi (still at 20 Fairmont Avenue, Ottawa) purchased land for the construction of a summer retreat and chapel. Père Alexis bought two acres from James Farrell for $40 on condition that his elderly mother could take Sunday Mass with the Capucins — this instead of having to go to Old Chelsea. The brothers built a dormitory here, to which they walked, leaving their Ottawa parish church at midnight for the trip. The 24.5 km walk took five hours to O'Brien Beach, where one — perhaps Father Bernardin Boucher — would wave his arms until a cottager came by to transport them to the chapel. If no one came, they walked the last few kilometres along the path you walk today.

During the years when the retreat was in frequent use, many Meech Lake cottagers enjoyed summer evenings during which the Capucins would canoe on Meech Lake, singing their French hymns. Imagine how their voices must have echoed across the water.

More recently, cottagers have spun tales of the late prime minister, Pierre Elliott Trudeau, and how he would paddle to the chapel from Lac Mousseau with his young sons to attend service here when he could.

There used to be a wooden cross built on the hill overlooking Hope Bay, commemorating a Capucin who drowned. Father Bernardin wrote to me in 1991, explaining the death:

> Once a year those students paid a visit to the Dominican students at Deschênes Lake by boat. On July 4, 1934 they paid their annual visit. On the way back they were late, and one boat at least was overcrowded … and old. The water had slowly seeped in and the boat sank maybe ten feet from the shore — on the right side of Saint Anthony's statue. One student, Brother Joseph Marie Désautels, was drowned.

The Capucin Chapel, Meech Lake, showing statue of St. Anthony as carved by Victor Tolgyesy. 1985. Photo: Katharine Fletcher.

E: McCLOSKEY

Hike/ski trail only: #2, #21 & #33
Shared/ski trail #40, #24, #1 (& #2 to Western)
7.5 km return
Allow 3 hours

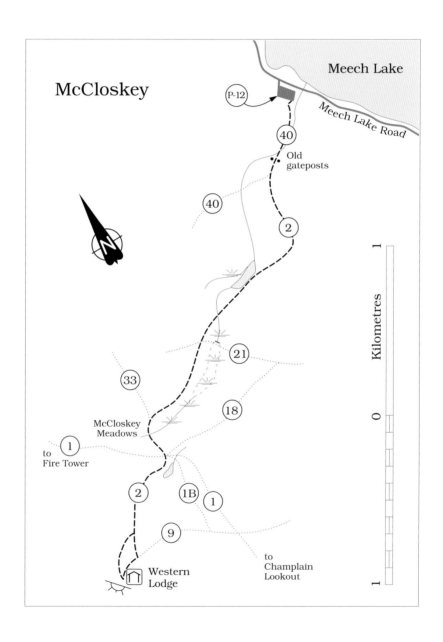

This very hilly hike climbs the steep ridge from Meech Lake to Western Lodge via the McCloskey Meadows. The lodge rewards you with a cozy shelter on a cool day, complete with wood stove which Park staff keeps well-supplied with wood. The view from the Eardley Escarpment to the Mountain Road and Ottawa Valley below is breathtaking and there is good bird watching from your aerie perch. Canoeing is excellent on Meech Lake, just beware: it's a big lake and whitecaps can whip up quickly.

Access: From Old Chelsea take the Meech Lake Road until you reach Meech lot, P-12 (between O'Brien Beach, P-11, and P-13, at Blanchet Beach). The very narrow, winding road beside the lake has no shoulders; take care when driving and watch out for children. **Note:** A fee is in effect in summer.

Facilities: Outhouses (at beach and lodge), garbage bins and (unless vandalized) a ski trail map posted at the base of the ridge at P-12 and at Western Lodge; wood stove at the lodge. Swimming, canoeing, and windsurfing at Meech Lake (bring your own gear). The ski is an exhilarating rush. This is an uphill pull via #2 and the meadows are open to the sun; in summer especially, take lots to drink and wear a wide-brimmed hat.

Trail description: The trailhead is at the southeastern tip of P-12. Head straight up ski trail #40, MacDonald Road. The trail forks 100 metres past an old gate, and #40 veers off to the right. In this walk description I describe the very steep trail #2 (to avoid the steep ascent, go right on #40, which the NCC has recently restored, and loop back to the McCloskey Meadows by veering right on Bradley, #33 and then on #21.)

Stay left on #2, and continue uphill, noting the stream that criss-crosses your path. After about 1 km, Pipe Dream, #21, appears: stay on #2. Just past the intersection you see a wetland (former beaver pond). When I started studying the trails for the first guide in 1985, this was a very active beaver pond complete with lodge.

The climb levels here. Soon you emerge into the McCloskey Meadows. Trail #33 points 3 km to Meech Lake, to your right. Stay on #2: a sign also points the way to Western Lodge, 1 km. Continue on #2. You are in the McCloskey clearing, with tall grasses and lilac bushes on your right. (**Tip:** Lilacs are a clue to homestead sites; this is where the McCloskey's house was.) After about 250 metres more, Ridge Road, #1, appears, and a signpost points .5 km to Western Lodge.

View from Western Lodge of Ottawa River and the flat Ottawa Valley plain, with Mountain Road in the foreground.
Photo: Katharine Fletcher, August 1987.

Cross Ridge Road and stay right, on #2 to the lodge. You pass by another clearing. (**Tip:** In the old pasture find a pile of rocks beside a hawthorn tree. Look for garter snakes sunning themselves.) Return to #2 and plunge into the cool hardwood forest. Immediately look for old stone walls as you descend from clearing to woodland. Just before you get to Western Lodge a fork in the trail appears (see map). Go left or right: both lead a few more metres to the lodge. To return, retrace your steps. Hot? Go for a swim in Meech Lake.

Intersecting trails:

#40 MacDonald Road: Newly redone by the NCC, this is a lovely loop alternative, with Bradley, #33, and/or Pipe Dream, #21: why not explore?

#1 Ridge Road: intersects with #9. Could form alternate circuit (see map).

#9 Western: only use as a possible circuit, connecting to Ridge Road.

Points of interest: The old clearings give free reign to your imagination. Look for piles of lichen-covered rocks, and imagine how difficult they were to pry from unforgiving, scant topsoil. Settlers put them on stoneboats, then the patient horse or ox hauled them to a designated spot where they were unloaded in the piles you see today. Hot, hard work for man and beast. The McCloskeys were some of the original settlers to move up the mountain, eking out a subsistence-level farming operation in the thin soil of the ridge in the mid 1800s. Later on, their farmhouse offered food and shelter to many Ottawa Ski Club members. In Marshall's book *The History of the Ottawa Ski Club*, there is a photograph of skiers in front of the McCloskey barn.

McCloskey Trail passes through hardwood forest and old farmland, providing an excellent lookout over the wide Ottawa River Valley as its final reward. On the long haul up the ridges keep a sharp eye open in late May for jack-in-the-pulpits found in the damp earth along the streambed. In the meadows look for honeysuckle, lilac, phlox, and Canada anemone; in the alders and woods bordering the meadows watch for deer. Bird watching is excellent. At the forest verge be alert for the blue flash of an indigo bunting.

Tilley residence, cottage on Meech Lake, n.d.
NCC historical files 05.0081000.0164

F: WOLF TRAIL

Hike/ski/snowshoe trail: #16
8.3 km return
Allow 3 hours

This very steep hike climbs from Meech Lake to a fabulous lookout over the Ottawa Valley. From here you can see Ghost Hill at Breckenridge. It also gives you great lookouts "into" the park itself, which is rare. Take binoculars. In summer, cool off at Meech Lake, which beckons you for a swim or even a canoe ride, after your strenuous hike.

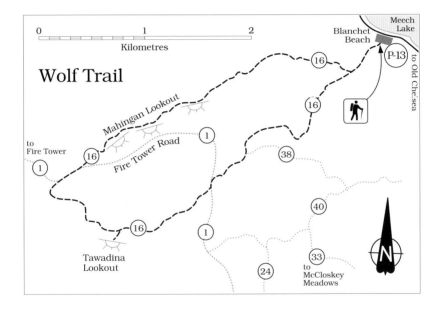

Access: From Old Chelsea take the Meech Lake Road until you reach Blanchet, P-13. **Note:** Because of beach access there is a fee in summer.

Facilities: Outhouses (at beach), garbage bins and (unless vandalized) a ski trail map at the base of the ridge at P-13. Swimming, canoeing and windsurfing at Meech Lake (bring your own gear). Note this is a red ski trail.

Trail description: The trailhead is near the southwest end of P-13. Immediately ascend trail #16 past thimbleberry, raspberry, and clumps of maidenhair fern. After about 500 metres you come to a fork: stay left; after 400 metres you cross a small stream. At the beaver pond, look left: can you see the bear claw marks in the beech tree? Proceed another kilometre and you see trail #38 heading left: remain on #16 (right). After almost 600 metres more you find Ridge Road (#1), sometimes called the Fire Tower Road. You have climbed 2.5 km.

Stay straight on #16. You climb another kilometre past a small black cherry grove (some of the trees have interesting burls) to Tawadina Lookout over the Ottawa Valley. As you climb this last kilometre, notice how the vegetation dramatically alters from northern-facing mixed woods to the stunted oaks of the escarpment edge. Across the Ottawa River can you spy Kanata?

Bear claw marks on smooth bark of an American Beech tree. Photo: Katharine Fletcher, October 1988.

Now start the return loop. You must now stay left on #16 to complete your circuit. The footing is first rocky here, then gets rather wet until you reach a rocky outcrop in the trail, with young black cherry and spruce. Then you get to a bog: a wonderful beaver pond complete with lodge. I found salamander eggs here once; explore a bit. Wander past blueberries, touch-me-nots, and iris. 1.4 km after Tawadina Lookout you arrive at Ridge Road, #1, again. Cross it to stay on #16. You soon get to a series of three amazing lookouts, collectively called "Mahingan" (Wolf), giving you a view east, into the park. Below, you will see beaver ponds. Continue your sometimes steep descent through a hemlock grove and beside more old ponds with blue vervain, hawkweed, boneset, and arrowhead. After the hemlocks it's another kilometre to the first fork, which completes the circuit of #16. Stay left, now, and sharply descend to Blanchet. Tired? Hot? Head for a swim at Meech Lake: you deserve it.

Intersecting trails:

#38: Connects with MacDonald Road, trail #40, and from there to McCloskey, and more.

#1 Ridge Road: goes west to the fire tower atop Luskville Falls via McKinstrey Lodge and interconnects with many routes.

Points of interest: Wolf Trail has become "the" favourite trail of the park. It is extremely beautiful, gives you a strenuous workout, and rewards you with a stunning view of our Ottawa Valley.

At Tawadina ("Valley" in Algonquin) try to find settler Joseph Lusk's Ghost Hill Farm in the valley below: look east on Highway 148. Find the terraced edge of the valley, marked by the dark swath of evergreens. This steep and twisting road (now straightened) was home to many a "haunt." Tales of murder, hidden treasure, and the elusive will o' the wisp abound there, at the steep descent to Breckenridge. Mahingan Lookout is gorgeous in autumn's colours as it looks into the park itself. Can you see the Camp Fortune tower, or Morrisson's Quarry, at Wakefield?

G: SKYLINE

Hike/ski trails: #30 & #6
5 km return
Allow 2 hours

This scenic hike takes you to several outstanding lookouts over the skylines of Ottawa and Gatineau (formerly Hull). After the initial climb the trail remains elevated, although you stay in a hardwood forest for most of the walk. Views are best

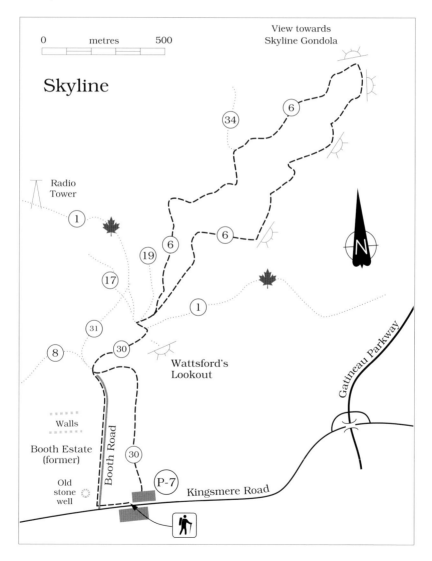

in early spring or autumn so the leaves don't block the view. Skyline trail #6 is strictly a hike/ski trail whereas #30 is shared. Note that Skyline forms a complete circuit of its own.

Access: Take the Old Chelsea turnoff on Highway #5. Go left on Kingsmere Road. Park at P-7.

Facilities: Outhouses, garbage bins, one or possibly two interpretive signs; several outstanding lookouts over the cities of Ottawa/Gatineau.

Trail description: Note: You will return on trail #30 at the north side of the parking lot but to avoid having to double back, this hike starts with an interesting diversion. From the parking lot, face Kingsmere Road and turn right. Watch for traffic as you walk the few paces to Booth Road. On your right appears the Crannell house, set well back from the road behind rock walls. Turn right on Booth Road. Almost immediately on your left you'll notice two sets of stone pillars marking the circular driveway of Opeongo, the former J.R. Booth estate, now neglected and overgrown. Once the well-kept Booth Picnic Field, the NCC no longer maintains it.

As you pass alongside the old Booth estate, why not explore it? You will discover the two old stone retaining walls, wild-looking remnants of J.R. Booth's orchard, and, at the southeast section of the property, an old "wishing well." **Tip:** Watch out for poison ivy near the well.

Continue walking for now, noting the very mature white pines ahead on your left and, in July and August, the thick carpet of blossoming creeping thyme that turns the fields a mauve colour. Soon the gravel Booth Road ends and the trail slips into the forest. Stay left on the main path (#30) as it begins to climb. Within a few metres, at the junction with #8 (Highland), turn sharply right and after another 300 metres uphill, you connect with Ridge Road, #1, which is part of the Trans-Canada Trail here. Wattsford's lookout is a few metres immediately to your right. After admiring the view of Ottawa's skyline, ascend a few more metres up Ridge Road to meet Skyline Trail, #6, and turn right. Skyline can be somewhat confusing because you'll come to a few minor trails veering off to the right. If you take these, you'll find the Camp Fortune ski slopes whose clear cuts afford tremendous views of the countryside. Walkers and bikers use the ski hills in summer.

However, this trail description keeps you on #6 throughout. Therefore, once on Skyline, keep to your right to complete the loop.

The elevation throughout is reasonably level. The first half of the trail winds through a mixed hardwood/softwood forest and presents several lookouts, some of which give better views than others through the trees. Views include: Cité des Jeunes; Highway 105; Highway 5; Gatineau River; mills in Gatineau East. Two of these lookouts were named "Lone Pine" and "The Lakes" on a 1957 FDC map. You'll also find an interpretive sign explaining how #6 was built in 1938 as a Depression era relief project, plus you will see frequent remnants of stone embankment walls.

On the second half of the loop, the trail passes through a hemlock woods (these trees usually grow on a northern slope). But other trees are well represented, too: beech trees (look for the impression of bear claws on their smooth bark) and yellow birch are particularly attractive.

Return to your car after completing the Skyline Circuit by retracing your steps down the hill of #30 from Wattsford's Lookout. Instead of following the gravel road, stay left on #30 to return to P-7.

Intersecting trails: several

#8 Highland: heads southwest from #30 below Wattsford's Lookout. It continues west to parallel the Champlain Parkway before heading northwest to connect with Nature, #17, and Ridge Road.

#1 Ridge Road: this is the major trail with which you intersect at Wattsford's Lookout. To the east it sharply descends first to the Penguin Picnic Ground (1.5 km) and then to the Old Chelsea Picnic Ground (2 km) and Visitor's Centre (3.5 km); to the west it passes by a fascinating beaver pond. Ridge Road passes Survey trail heading north to the Camp Fortune telecommunication tower. It also intersects with Fortune Lane (#4) descending to both Fortune and Alexander lodges at the ski hills. If you continue west on Ridge Road, you eventually get to Champlain Lookout and the Western Sector of Gatineau Park — a long hike of about 18 km return.

Points of interest: J.R. Booth, one of Ottawa's famous lumber barons, started his career as a carpenter for Andrew Leamy, at his sawmill at Leamy Creek circa 1850. Booth soon rented and then purchased a sawmill — the start to a successful entrepreneurial career in lumber. The Booth estate grounds were once J.R. Booth's Kingsmere Lake summer retreat, a residence he named Opeongo. The aerial photograph

Aerial view of Kingsmere Lake, showing clearings circa 1930. The J.R. Booth estate (demolished) is at bottom right with circular driveway. Note abrupt escarpment edge with flat Ottawa Valley below, Ottawa River in background. NAC PA–126165.

on page 116 shows the estate: it's marked by the "doughnut-shaped" circular drive at the bottom right. Use this photo to orient yourself when you explore the property; you can approximate where the stone pillars marking the former driveways were. Can you see the "grid" shape denoting "J.R.'s orchard?"

Skyline hike emphasizes the major significance that the Ottawa Ski Club has had on developing the trails. The Club was formed in 1910, graduating from what was first a focus on ski-jumping to cross-country and then to downhill skiing. Its members carved a network of elaborate trails, ski hills, and lodges throughout the eastern section of the park. The club leased land from the NCC in the early sixties to create Skyline ski hills. This was announced in the Club's Yearbook of 1959–60 "the major development was the opening of what had once been Bud Clark's Ski School area, facing north and sloping down to Meach [sic] Lake Road. It became, under the aegis of the Ottawa Ski Club, the new Skyline slopes. John Clifford Ski Tows furnished it with a poma lift. The first section of a new lodge was erected on top of the ridge."[71]

Between 1932 and 1960, downhill skiing fever swept the Gatineau and, according to an old map, in 1940 the first ski tow commenced operation. In the early 1960s, Camp Fortune was one of the first clubs to experiment with the latest in skiing technology: artificial snow-making equipment. In 1991 the NCC bought 168 hectares comprising Camp Fortune and now a private company operates it under a twenty-five-year lease. Skyline Hill has two chairlifts and come autumn one is employed offering scenic "gondola rides" showcasing the fall colours.

John Dunlop was one of the first settlers of this area, building his home here in the early 1860s. The road named after him, Dunlop Road, can be seen from the downhill runs descending to Camp Fortune, which got its name from pioneer Garrett Fortune.

Note: Mountain biking is popular at Camp Fortune. However, while some of the cross-country trails developed on this property do connect, they are not integrated with the park's network. Note that Skyline trail is not a shared trail: absolutely no biking is permitted on it.

J.R. Booth mansion. Note the stone wall: Booth helped to select the rocks. NCC historical file D14–45.

H: MOORE

Handicapped access
4-season hiking trail: #35
2 km
Allow 1.5 hr

Explore the historic estate of former Prime Minister King's former home, Moorside, and his 1903 cottage, Kingswood. Here you'll find some of the stately white pines for which the Ottawa Valley became famous in the heyday of the timber barons. Beautiful gardens, museums, and King's romantic collection of ruins will bring you back to Moorside again and again.

Access: The trailhead is found at Moorside, the Mackenzie King Estate. As of Autumn 2003, the official access to the Mackenzie King Estate is from the Champlain Parkway. Some conservationists were indignant when the NCC cut this new swath through the woods from the parkway to the parking lot at Moorside. But the NCC persevered, adding this new road within the park boundaries so that visitors can access the estate without congesting the municipal roads (Kingsmere, Swamp, and Barnes). Residents living along these roads had been complaining for years about the increased traffic–and once again, the NCC was caught in the middle. To find this new road, simply turn onto the Champlain Parkway from the Gatineau Parkway: the road leading to the estate is well signed, appearing on your right (north). Note that after the parkways are closed for the winter, all-season access to the estate still is available via Old Chelsea, and Kingsmere, Swamp, and Barnes roads. A fee still applies at P6, the Mackenzie King Parking Lot.

Facilities: One trail that extends from the parking lot to Moorside is paved. The pavement continues past the toilet facilities to the Abbey Ruins. During the summer season, museums at Kingswood and Moorside are open and interpretive staff and videos are available. (Confirm whether the Moorside Tearoom is open past the summer months by calling the Old Chelsea Visitor's Centre.)

Moorside, Kingsmere, 1927. NAC PA–124733.

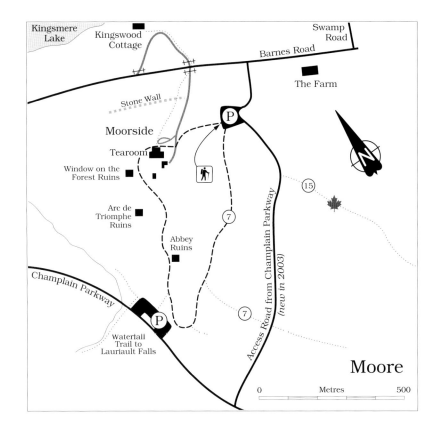

Trail description: After alighting from your car, find the paved path leading west to Moorside. Stop and read interpretive sign about King. Continue to the gravel driveway; turn left towards Moorside. Old stone walls, originally built by Paddy Murphy of Old Chelsea, define the walkways and pastures of the estate. (**Note:** Turn right to Kingswood Cottage.) If open, enter Moorside: a flight of stairs inside the main door takes you to the tiny museum. Return outside to the spacious gardens. The NCC has restored these formal gardens to the way they were between 1928 and 1933.

Now start to explore King's famous collection of ruins. Particularly inspired by eighteenth century English romantic notions of creating "picturesque views," King spent hours and sleepless nights worrying over their specific placement and design. The first set of ruins, Window on the Forest, serves as focal point to the flower beds. Erected in 1936, the stones are from Ottawa's demolished British North America (BNA) Bank Note building. To the right, find the path to the Hidden Garden, a re-creation of King's 1933 rock garden. Return to the formal gardens; turn right.

At a spot King called Diana's Grove, after the Greek goddess of the hunt, you'll find the second ruin, Arc de Triomphe, built in 1936 from the pillared entryway salvaged from the same BNA building. Proceed up the rise to King's most famous creations, his 1935–37 Abbey Ruins. Some stones are from the home of former Quebec premier Simon Napoleon Parent, others from the original Centre Block of Ottawa's parliament buildings, destroyed in the February 3, 1916 fire. King hired architect J. Albert Ewart (who designed the Civic Hospital among other buildings) to help design the Abbey Ruins. An incurable romantic, King buried his Irish terrier Pat I here at the Abbey Ruins, instructing the gardener to plant fragrant creeping thyme (which has truly spread) to mark the grave. King often read poetry by the grave, amid the ruins he named after England's famous Tintern and Melrose abbeys.

Proceed down the paved trail that rather plummets downhill. Now veer sharply left at the fork in Moore trail, (blue ski trail #35), to your car at P-6.

Intersecting trails:

#7 Dennison: If you continue on #35 instead of veering left to return to your car at P-6, you connect with trail #7. You can wander down this trail a ways, bypassing a "beaver pond lake" before it connects to P-7. It is wet.

Former Prime Minister King, with Irish terrier Pat at Moorside, n.d. NAC C–24304.

Abbey Ruins, Moorside. NAC PA–129853.

Points of interest: There is much to see and do at Moorside, a portion of the former prime minister's 231 hectare estate. Don't forget to explore Kingswood Cottage, just a bit further north on Barnes Road. It is fully interpreted and open to the public in summer.

There are innumerable tales of King and his romanticized, Victorianesque love for Kingsmere. Although he used Moorside as a retreat, he frequently entertained guests here. Often such visits inspired anecdotes about the prime minister. On one occasion, after inviting Sir Ronald and Lady Storr to join him for dinner, King discovered his pantry was bare. Fortunately his dear friends the Pattesons, who lived just next door, were renowned for:

> … the serving of sumptuous meals. Neighbour King hastened across the field.

> The Patteson kitchen door stood open, giving off a gratifying smell of roast beef. Mrs. Patteson had just put the roast on a serving platter. Much to her surprise, Neighbour Rex — as she

called him — suddenly entered, picked up the platter and, with no time to explain, invited Mr. and Mrs. Patteson to come over to have dinner with him ...

They followed in procession across the field, with Yorkshire pudding, gravy, vegetable and whatever else they could load on trays.[72]

Another resident, Willy Murphy of Kingsmere, recalled that King used to practise public speaking while hiking through the woods. Perhaps, as you linger at the Abbey Ruins, you'll catch a line or two of poetry near Pat's grave ...

Today the lake is still surrounded by private residences: in fact there are seventy-one homes in the community. Sixty-four are permanent homes, whereas seven are cottages. An additional thirty lots could potentially be severed for buildings, which gives one food for thought concerning parks and their use.

1: PINK LAKE AND HERMIT

Shared bike/hike/ski trail: #15 & #5
12 km return
Allow 5 hours

Pink Lake is an ecological treasure (no, it's not pink — it's meromitic) whose name commemorates an Irish immigrant family. Hermit Trail is named after Miles Barnes, the recluse who lived near Barnes Road. There are two possible all-season trailheads to this lovely walk and lake: I recommend starting at Moorside, Mackenzie King's Estate. However, you could also start at Mine Road using trail #5 to connect to #15, part of the Trans-Canada Trail (see map). During the summer you can park at either Pink Lake parking lot and do as much walking as you wish. Cycling is not permitted on the boardwalk around Pink Lake.

Access: All season: Start from Moorside parking lot (fee for parking applies in summer). From Hull take Highway #5 to Old Chelsea and turn left on Kingsmere Road. Go left on Swamp Road, then right on Barnes Road. The parking lot is on your left. Park here. **Note:** When the parkways are open, drive up Gatineau Parkway to Pink Lake. There are two Pink Lake lots (see map). Note also the summer access road to Moorside from the Champlain Parkway. Cyclists can access trail #5 from Mine Road.

Facilities: At Moorside there are toilets, garbage bins, a snack bar, tearoom, and a museum, variously, in season; at Pink Lake's two parking lots there are garbage bins and an outhouse as well as interpretive signs and a boardwalk around the lake; the Mine Road access has no parking lot, no facilities. **Note:** Do not swim in Pink Lake. It is ecologically fragile.

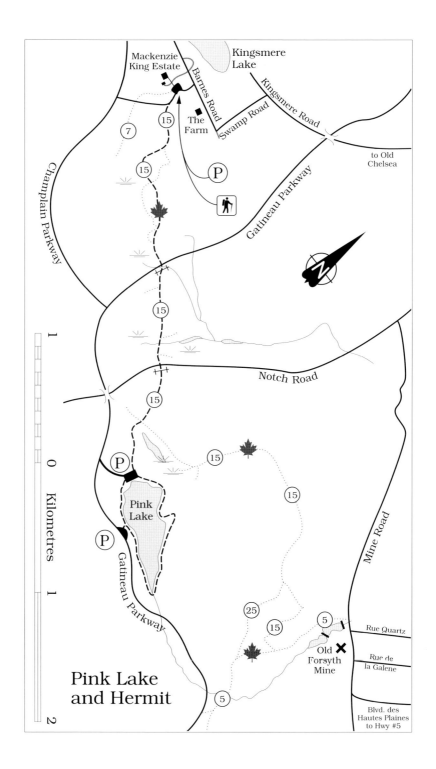

Mackenzie
King Estate

Kingsmere
Lake

⑦

⑮

Barnes Road

The
Farm

Swamp Road

Kingsmere Road

Champlain Parkway

⑮

Ⓟ

🚶

Gatineau Parkway

to Old
Chelsea

Ⓝ

⑮

⑮

Notch Road

1

Ⓟ

⑮

⑮

Mine Road

Kilometres

0

Pink
Lake

Ⓟ

1

Gatineau Parkway

㉕

⑮

⑤

Rue Quartz

2

⑮

Old
Forsyth
Mine

✕

Rue de
la Galène

Pink Lake
and Hermit

⑤

Blvd. des
Hautes Plaines
to Hwy #5

Trail description: Find trail #15 at the southeast corner of the Moorside parking lot. The trail soon forks: #15 is on your left, #7 is to your right. Keep to your left on #15, part of the Trans-Canada Trail. Stay on #15 as it wends its way through the woods to its intersection with the Gatineau Parkway, about 1.75 km; then proceed 1 km to its junction with Notch Road. It is about 300 metres from Notch Road to the fork in the trail. To get to Pink Lake, stay straight and continue another 300 metres to the lower parking lot where you connect with the boardwalk circling the lake. Excellent interpretive signs inform you about its meromitic qualities as you walk around it.

To return to your car, backtrack to Moorside.

Intersecting trails: Several old trails intersect #15 and #5. Check out the NCC summer trails map: you can continue along trail #5 to #29, or remain on #5 to connect eventually with St. Raymond, Gamelin, and Taché boulevards.

Points of interest: Pink Lake is a rare meromitic lake, one in which the water never has a chance to mix, resulting in a stratified series of "layers." In most lakes, water circulates, movement is important so that oxygen and nutrients can mix. Pink Lake's steep sides protect it from wind so that only the top thirteen metres actually mix. The

The beginning of the boardwalk around Pink Lake, July 2002.
Photo: Eric Fletcher.

bottom "layer" is seven metres deep, being completely without oxygen. Primitive anaerobic bacteria, which transform sunlight into the energy they need, live at the top of this layer and form a dense cloud that prevents light from reaching the bottom of Pink Lake.

Because the bottom layer has no oxygen, it provides a fascinating "core slice" of history. Why? Without oxygen and light, vegetable matter such as pollen that falls into the lake never decomposes. Therefore, samples taken from the bottom of Pink Lake provide an intriguing glimpse into the lake's natural history, giving insights into such things as the amount of lead in the air, or when forest fires occurred.

Why does Pink Lake resemble those green-coloured lakes in western Canada? Because of eutrophication, a natural process where oxygen is consumed by vegetation such as algae. Phosphorous, which is plentiful in the surrounding cliffs, acts like a natural fertilizer that primitive plants such as algae thrive upon. Before the NCC's four-year rehabilitation program was completed in 1991, people enjoyed climbing the rocks encircling the lake and diving into the water. As they clambered over the rocks, phosphorous tumbled into Pink Lake, initiating a chain of events. Too much phosphorous resulted in algal blooms, which led to oxygen depletion … which killed fish and other lake organisms.

Many park visitors dislike boardwalks, but as we can see here at Pink Lake, there is good reason for them: it's all about conservation and preservation of habitats. As you walk on the boardwalks and read the signs at the viewing platforms, note the young trees planted by volunteers to prevent further erosion.

If you wish, you can walk from Pink Lake to Mine Road along trails #15 and #5, a one-way distance of 3.9 km. Look for deer or fox in the open areas. At the reservoir you may see ducks, muskrat, leopard frogs, or perhaps a great blue heron fishing for tadpoles. The reservoir has its stories: one hiker told me he recollects wintry days when teams of horses and men went onto the frozen water to cut ice in days before refrigeration. He told me exciting stories of long ago, of previous land-owners, and of the house of ill repute hidden in the woods nearby …

J: HICKORY TRAIL

Handicapped access
Unnumbered hike/ski trail
500 metres
Allow 15 minutes

This safe, flat trail is superb for children and the elderly, who have special needs. The path goes through two types of woods in Gatineau Park: younger evolving woods and established mixed maple and hickory stands.

Access: Take Gatineau Parkway from Gamelin Boulevard in Hull. Stay on this parkway until you see the Hickory Trail parking lot appear on your left. Park here.

Facilities: There are toilets and picnic tables.

Trail description: This is an easy circuit with numbered interpretive signs. **Please note:** I have not included a map for this hike as the path is well marked.

Intersecting trails: None.

Points of interest: Named for the bitternut hickory tree, this easy walk is an excellent introduction to Gatineau Park. The story of the Hickory Trail is one of succession: in this case, of how land once cleared is gradually reclaimed by nature. Find the erratic, a large boulder left behind as the glacier receded. Birders may find the black-billed cuckoo here, notably during tent caterpillar season.

K: LAURIAULT FALLS & MULVIHILL LAKE

Unnumbered hike/ski trail
3 km return
Allow 1 hour

Lauriault Trail traverses quiet hardwood forests, where towering maple trees form a majestic canopy overhead. Lookouts provide excellent views over the Ottawa Valley; a pretty waterfall beckons you in spring … and a meandering stream beside the footpath accompanies you. You can take a diversion to Moorside, part of the Mackenzie King Estate.

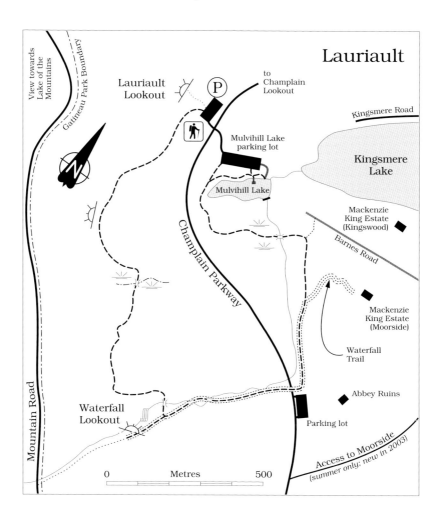

Access: Drive northwest on Gatineau Parkway, past Hickory Trail and Pink Lake. Turn left at the Champlain Parkway, and after 3 km find Mulvihill Lake on your right. (You will have passed the new road into Mackenzie King Estate and its lower parking lot.) Directly opposite, find Lauriault parking lot and picnic ground. Park there.

Facilities: There are outhouses, picnic tables, and garbage cans at both the Lauriault and Mulvihill Lake parking lots. The Mulvihill Lake trails are all paved and a sturdy wooden wharf allows easy access to the water.

Trail description: The trailhead is directly opposite the entrance to the Lauriault parking lot, to your left as you drive in. (**Hint:** You may wish to start by taking an immediate diversion to a lookout over the Ottawa Valley. Veer to the right from the trailhead and go straight to the escarpment edge. From here you can see the Lake of the Mountains. Join the main trail by heading to your left for about 50 metres.)

At the trailhead, the path immediately curves left, gently ascending to a lookout over the Ottawa River Valley below. Just after you set out, look right: can you find some old foundations? Now proceed left, starting a gradual descent through the wooded slopes of the mountainside. Keep your eyes peeled for an immense erratic to your left, a huge boulder left behind as the glacier melted. Continue up a couple of wooden stairs that negotiate some rough spots, until you suddenly become aware of the sound of the stream. After crossing a wooden bridge over the creek you arrive at a fork in the trail. Turn right and descend steeply to the stone-walled lookout over Lauriault Falls on your right. This viewing area makes a pleasant spot to sit down, take a well-deserved rest, and absorb the quiet beauty of the woods.

Return uphill to the fork and stay straight on the Waterfall Trail (turn left back onto Lauriault Trail to retrace your steps to the car if you wish). Here the gurgling stream criss-crosses the path until you arrive at the tunnel beneath the Champlain Parkway. Go through the tunnel.

On the far side of it, veer left, staying on the wide trail. Your path goes straight, past two small trails that head off to the right. (The first ascends to the Moorside Estate, passing a cave that was another natural formation that intrigued King. The second path goes to Barnes Road and Kingswood Cottage.) Continue on the main trail, which eventually curves to the left, crosses a little bridge over a swampy spot, and climbs the last, short hill to Mulvihill Lake. Watch for smooth, grey-barked American beech at the start of this hill: a few of them are what I call "bear trees" because they have permanent claw marks. Black bears clamber up to munch on beech nuts in autumn, leaving the imprint of their claws in the smooth bark.

Intersecting trails: No major intersections save the two trails mentioned above.

Points of interest: This walk is steeped in local history. The Mulvihills were settlers in the mid 1800s. John Mulvihill arrived in Bytown in 1828 and worked as a clerk in the Hundredth Regiment. Michael Mulvihill, his grandson, had a home on Kingsmere Road near the lake that bears the family name.

Originally, Kingsmere Road descended "Lauriault's Hill" down to the Mountain Road, but it was closed in 1957. Today this location is marked by a sign, "The Hollow."

Mulvihill Lake was created by Bud Mulvihill who bulldozed it out of the earth in 1948. The property was adjacent to King, who started a lawsuit against his neighbour, complaining about the building of the dam and creation of the lake. Among other things, King was concerned about the impact on his beloved waterfall. On the north side of Mulvihill Lake parking lot, a flattened area of ground is carpeted in summer by domestic pinks. A broken-down stone retaining wall suggests that this was the site of Bud Mulvihill's cabin. Barnes Road is named after the hermit Miles Barnes, who had a small orchard and cabin hereabouts.

After purchasing three parcels of land that the stream and falls traversed, King designed the trail leading from Moorside to the falls, starting in the late 1920s. He contributed to local employment by hiring teams of men and horses — and, later, bulldozers — to widen the path and build bridges. As you walk, you tread in the footsteps of Winston Churchill and Lord Tweedsmuir, for King loved to take his guests to his "Bridal Veil" falls.

L: KING MOUNTAIN & BLACK LAKE

Unnumbered hiking trail
NCC interpreted trail
2.5 km return
Allow 1 hour

The view of the Ottawa Valley from King Mountain is superb on a clear day. It's a favourite destination for geographical field trips, because the geology of the rift valley is visible here. How has geology affected human development? How many human uses of the landscape can you see? Here, too, the microclimate of the Eardley Escarpment can be closely examined.

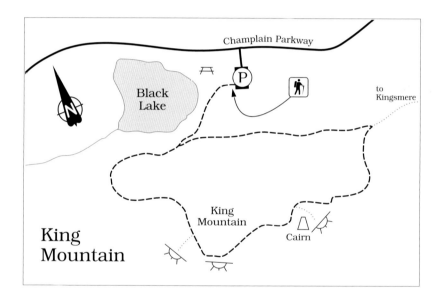

Access: Take the Champlain Parkway for roughly 5 km from the Gatineau Parkway. King Mountain/Black Lake parking lot is on your left. Park here.

Facilities: There are outhouses, picnic tables, and barbecue facilities. An NCC booklet and information panel describe the microclimate of the Eardley Escarpment.

Trail description: The trailhead is on the west side of the parking lot, past the outhouses. The path descends the hill to Black Lake. Veer right on the path beside the lake until you see the sharp rise in the trail heading left, through the hemlock woods on the north, shaded slope of King Mountain. Before leaving the lake, pause for a moment. Take in the views: is there a blue heron? Can you see some blue flag wild iris? Is there a beaver today? Now start a steep ascent up sturdy stairs built here to prevent soil erosion. **Note:** Don't contribute to erosion: stay on the boardwalk.

King (second from left) and "Mr. Skelton" at King Mountain,
July 29, 1923. NAC C–2130.

A dramatic change in the woods announces that the summit is near. Hemlock-covered northern slopes give way to a hardwood maple and beech wood. Soon you emerge at the first of three main lookouts facing south over the Ottawa River Valley. Here you get an excellent view of Lake of the Mountains below. Look for signs of human use of the land: settlement, transport, quarries, farming: there is a lot to see and discuss here. You can see white and red oak and an occasional juniper clinging to the rocky cliff face. Once back on the trail you soon reach the second lookout, with more splendid views.

Continue east to the third major lookout point where there is a large stone cairn. The cityscape of Ottawa and Gatineau extends below you, encroaching on the countryside. Proceed east and you will be rewarded with your final viewpoint before plunging back inside the woodland canopy. Here you start to descend King Mountain into towering woods of mature beech and maple. You have now almost completed the walk. Off to your right you pass an unnumbered trail pointing to Kingsmere. Continue walking (it's wet in places) and after a steep ascent you see Black Lake. The parking lot is on the right.

Intersecting trails: An unnumbered trail pointing to Kingsmere eventually connects to #8 and #6 (see map).

Points of interest: King Mountain is not named after the former prime minister. In fact, its origins are not precisely known — it's name could simply indicate that this is the biggest mountain in the area, or it could be named for an early settler, John King. Many claim that the stone cairn atop the mountain, which commemorates the 1905 start of the Geodetic Survey of Canada, provides the clue. A plaque states, "Here was commenced the triangulation system of the Geodetic Survey of Canada, the basis of surveys for all purposes, topographical, engineering and cadastral." Former Kingsmere resident Arthur Bourinot gives another possible derivation: "The Cairn was the spot where the first triangulation system in Canada was started by Dr. W.F. King. I can remember as a boy seeing the surveyors' lanterns shining as they climbed the mountain path at night and then at the top the flashing signal." In the same article, Bourinot wrote about a thirty-foot high cedar cross that once distinguished the mountain, built by Martin Welsh who lived at "The Hollow" along the Mountain Road, at the foot of Lauriault's Hill:

> At one time there was on the top of King Mountain a huge red cross, just about where the cairn now stands, which could be seen for miles around ... It eventually rotted and fell over the cliff and was never re-erected. It was originally placed there through the efforts of the Reverend Father Maguire, parish priest at Old Chelsea, 1888 to 1891.[73]

Natural history is rich here: the trail illustrates changes in woodland vegetation due to aspect, soil, wind, and light. The 200 metre high, 30 km long cliff face of the Eardley Escarpment is the predominant topographic feature of the park, defining its southern boundary. The ancient roots of mountains once as high as the Rockies, the exposed gneiss and granite bedrock is home to cliff-nesting ravens. The walk reveals a broad range of plants, from the orange wood-lily, painted trillium, and showy lady's slipper of the hemlock woods, to the sedges and blue harebell, three-toothed cinquefoil, wild rose, columbine, and stunted oaks of the escarpment face.

The lookouts are excellent for bird watching. The red-tailed hawk, with its wild shriek, and the turkey vulture with its red, featherless head, are two "gliders" that frequent this area. Find a perch of your own and watch them soar on the updrafts of air swirling along the cliff face. Be quiet, be patient: the scurryings of a busy chipmunk or sight of a garter snake sunbathing on the rocks may reward you. **Tip:** Take your binoculars.

M: NATURE & SUGARLOAF ROCK

Unnumbered hike/ski trail
2.2 km return
Allow 1 hour

You get a superb view of Ottawa from the top of Sugarloaf —
a big rock outcrop of 359 metres elevation. Some of the low
areas are wet in spring but this hilly trail is fine during most of
the season. Watch out: it's a challenging ski.

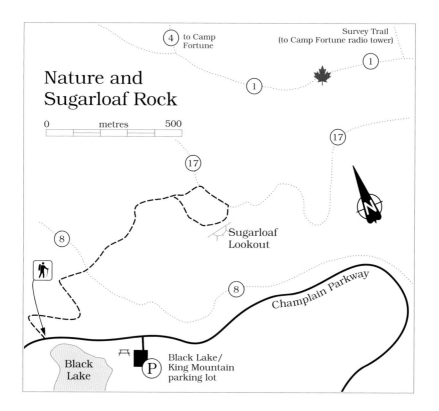

Nature and
Sugarloaf Rock

Access: Turn onto the Champlain Parkway from the Gatineau Parkway.
On your left find the Black Lake/King Mountain parking lot. Park here.

Facilities: Outhouses, picnic tables, and barbecues at Black Lake.

Trail description: From the parking lot, return to the Parkway and
walk west (left) until you are directly opposite the far end of Black
Lake (about 300 metres). Nature begins here on the opposite side of

the Champlain Parkway. Cross the road to reach the trailhead. **Note:** The NCC summer trail map depicts Nature (formerly #19) as a green hiking path connecting to Highland, #8. Continue uphill, following pronounced switchbacks for about 700 metres. Here you find trail #8, but you continue straight ahead on Nature.

After another 500 metres Sugarloaf Rock appears. Here Nature forks: the right-hand branch goes up Sugarloaf and the other around the left side of its base. Take the uphill branch and the short steep climb rewards you with an excellent view of Ottawa. Either return northwest down the hill the way you came, or continue on to circle around Sugarloaf.

At this dramatic rock's northeast base you may head off to the right on #17, until you join Ridge Road, #1, near Wattsford's Lookout (see Skyline walk). From there, you could follow #8 west back above the Parkway to where it rejoins Nature. Otherwise, follow #17 north for about 100 metres to where Nature turns off to the west (left). Follow it around the north side of Sugarloaf Rock to rejoin Nature and retrace your steps to the parkway and Black Lake.

Intersecting trails: Many destinations are possible from Nature if you continue as far as Ridge Road, #1. If you head northwest from Sugarloaf Rock you meet Fortune Lane, #4, going to Camp Fortune or else you can continue along #1 to Keogan Lodge or Champlain Lookout. Heading right (east) brings you to Survey. It goes north (left) to Camp Fortune radio tower. Further east, Ridge meets Skyline, Booth, Penguin, and Old Chelsea.

#8 Highland: heads east to trail #30 just above the Booth Estate. To the west it veers north to connect with Ridge Road just east of Lac Bourgeois.

Points of interest: Nature offers an excellent view of Ottawa and is a good scramble for children and adults. The area is rich in the history of the Ottawa Ski Club, the first group of people to open up and maintain trails of the Gatineau Park area for recreational skiing. Trail names here commemorate the Night Riders and the Trail Riders, men and women who worked hard on trail building and design as well as on maintenance and patrol. Sugarloaf Rock is so-named for its shape: in the olden days, sugar was made and purchased in loaf shapes, much like bread.

N: FORTUNE LAKE

Hike/ski trail: #32
1.5 km return
Allow .5 hour

This is a very short, easy walk particularly interesting for bird watching and pond life. It's also fun to canoe here: marshes are always fascinating. The area is most active in spring but it is enjoyable anytime.

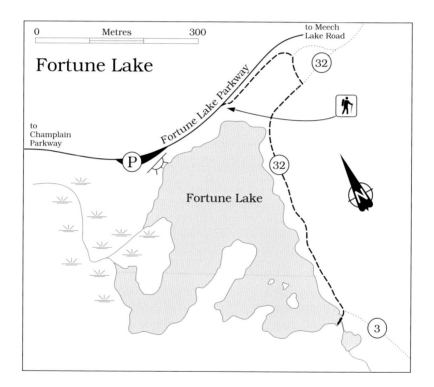

Access: From Old Chelsea take the Meech Lake Road. Turn left onto Fortune Lake Parkway. Keep to the right at the branch (Dunlop Road, to the left, leads to Camp Fortune). About 2.3 km up this road is a pullover overlooking Fortune Lake. Park here. Or, go up the Gatineau Parkway, turn left on the Champlain Parkway, then right onto Fortune Lake Parkway and the lake appears on your right. **Note:** Do not attempt to ski in winter on the surface of Fortune Lake because the ice is unstable. Nearby Camp Fortune pumps water from here for its facilities, rendering the ice unpredictable.

Facilities: A very small parking lot. It is not crowded most of the season; however, on weekends in the fall, when the coloured leaves attract crowds, it soon fills. Garbage bins here but no other facilities.

Trail description: Walk northeast on the Parkway for about 250 metres and turn right onto the trail. Take the left side of the trail as the right leads down to the lake. You soon come to trail #32. Turn right and follow the shore of Fortune Lake.

At the point where #32 ends and intersects with #3, turn right to Fortune Lake. There is an excellent view here complete with beautifully smooth rocks — have a seat and enjoy a picnic lunch, bird watching, or some sketching. You can see blue #3 ski trail markers going across the lake from here, tempting you to return for a winter experience.

Return by retracing your footsteps. The edge of the lake is too swampy to permit a circuit route.

Intersecting trails:

#32 Dulac: begins at the base of the Fortune Lake Parkway, paralleling the road up to Fortune Lake. (Dulac provides an alternate starting point for the hike — there is a parking lot at its trailhead.)

#3 Fortune: comes from Camp Fortune ski area about 1 km away. Beyond its intersection with #32 it crosses Fortune Lake, making it exclusively a winter ski trail. Near Étienne Brûlé Lookout, #3 becomes Burma Road Trail. **Note:** in winter you can connect to Keogan Lodge via trails #34, #14, and #1. See the NCC winter trail map.

Points of interest: The lake takes its name from Garrett Fortune, an early settler who had his cabin nearby, and after whom Camp Fortune is also named. Fortune Parkway was opened on October 3, 1956 by former Prime Minister Louis St. Laurent and a host of dignitaries including then Ottawa mayor, Charlotte Whitton.

Fortune is one of the prettiest lakes of the park, a favourite with artists who come to capture its beauty on canvas or film. It is a superb spot for observing wildlife. You may see rose-breasted or evening grosbeaks or a scarlet tanager in the woods. In the marsh, red-wing blackbirds sing, and several varieties of warbler build their nests. The woods are alive with red squirrels and chipmunks. Watch for painted turtles basking on logs as well as for muskrat and beaver. There is a man-made dam at the end of the lake as well as many signs of those other famous dam makers, the beaver.

Just beyond the east (left) side of the parking lot there is a way down to the lake. Put your canoe in here. **Note:** Never catch, remove, touch, or otherwise harm any wildlife.

O: BURMA ROAD & RAMPARTS

Hike/ski trails: #3 & #28
5.5 km return
Allow 2 hours

This hike takes you right across the spine-like ridge of the Park, from a southerly lookout (Étienne Brûlé) over the Ottawa Valley to a rocky outcrop romantically called Ramparts, overlooking Meech Lake.

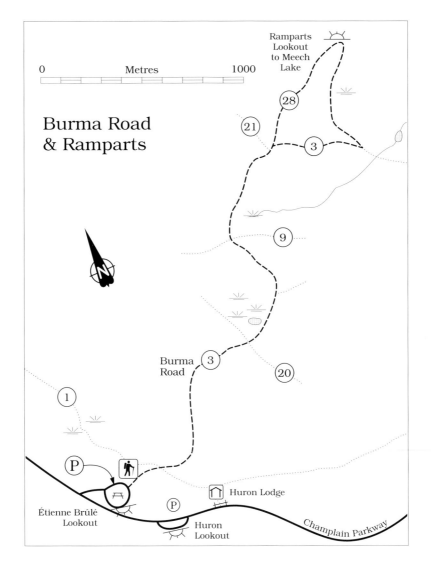

Access: Turn onto the Champlain Parkway from the Gatineau Parkway. Continue until you reach Étienne Brûlé Lookout and picnic ground to your right. Park here.

Facilities: Picnic and barbecue facilities, outhouses, and garbage bins.

Trail description: The trailhead is at the northeast side of the parking lot. Burma Road, #3, heads through the woods. After about 250 metres you cross Ridge Road. (You may soon see another faint trail, old #13, once known as Hidden Valley: stay on the main trail.) In another .75 km you cross #20, Pipe Dream. At this point, the trail enters marshy ground and gradually curves north. After almost .5 km you pass trail #9, Western. Stay on Burma Road. After about another 500 metres you intersect with #21, Huron.

Stay right on #3 for a few more metres and you will see another fork in the trail. Burma Road continues on ahead, but your new trail Ramparts, #28, goes sharply left. Follow Ramparts and after a 500 metre scramble up an overgrown section of trail, you emerge onto a rocky knoll overlooking Meech Lake. This is Ramparts Lookout.

View from northern shore of Meech Lake; note how much land used to be cleared at the turn of the century. The Tilley property, showing "Mother and Elsie," n.d. NAC C–80633.

To return, either backtrack or continue the loop formed by Ramparts, leading directly back to Burma Road, #3. At the fork, head to your right and retrace your steps to the Étienne Brûlé picnic ground.

Intersecting trails:

Many of the old paths along this walk had romantic-sounding names. for example, Hidden Valley used to lead to Keogan's Lodge near Fortune Lake. The NCC is rationalizing the trail network in the park and such trails are now unmarked and mostly forgotten. Please stay on the marked trails.

#1 Ridge Road: heads west to Western Lodge, the Lusk Cave, and Luskville Falls; goes east to Old Chelsea.

#20 Pipe Dream: connects with #9, and further west merges with #21, Huron Trail, just before joining up with #2, McCloskey, going to Meech Lake.

#9 Western: heads west to Western Lodge and extends as far east as the Fortune Lake Parkway.

#21 Huron: connects to #2, McCloskey, heading to Meech Lake.

Points of interest: This trail crosses the spine of Gatineau Park. The Ramparts Lookout over Meech Lake is especially good in early spring or late fall, when leafless trees permit a good view. However, during late spring and early summer, bird watching is excellent. On the rocks you are almost at eye level with the tree canopy. Here you may spot the exotic looking scarlet tanager in the treetops, or the lovely rose-breasted grosbeak. As you look out over Meech Lake, watch for a soaring osprey, turkey vulture, seagull, or red-tailed hawk.

Imagine how different a landscape this would have been in 1900, when the land was scarred from logging. By that time, there were several homesteaders at Meech Lake, including the Farrells who operated a farm. The Capucin Brothers built their chapel and retreat on a point at the lake in the early 1900s. Between 1907 and 1917 Thomas "Carbide" Willson built his home, boathouse, dam, generating station, and fertilizer plant here. Indeed, the lake was a hive of activity in days gone by, an activity that the tranquil cottages and NCC-operated beaches cannot match.

P: LODGE TOUR

Hike/ski trails: #1, #1B, #9 & #2
7 km
Allow 2.5 hours

This easy walking path introduces you to two Gatineau Park lodges, Western and Huron. Since the turn of this century, chalets have given refuge to cross-country skiers in the snows of winter, and during summer months provide a welcome site for picnics. Note that although trails #2, #1, and #1B are shared, #9 is not: bikers will need to avoid #9.

Access: After turning off the Gatineau onto the Champlain Parkway, pass the gated gravel lane to Huron Lodge on your right, and continue to Huron Lookout on your left. Park here.

Facilities: At both lodges you will find outhouses, picnic tables, and garbage containers.

Trail description: After parking, head right along the parkway. The trailhead is on the opposite side of the road. You'll see a gravel roadbed and a gate. Carefully cross the road, pass the gate, and ascend the short driveway.

After visiting the lodge, turn left on Ridge Road, #1. Walk along the wide path for 300 metres until you reach an intersection with Burma Road, #3. A signpost tells you it is 3 km to Western Lodge. (If you turn left here, you get to Ramparts — see Burma Road & Ramparts walk.) Continue straight along Ridge Road. You pass three major ponds that beavers created. The path dips and loops and you get pretty views: it's easy to lose a half-hour or so, lingering to watch for birds, frogs or beavers. Stay on #1 until you arrive at the intersection of the gravelled Ridge Road. You have gone about 1 km and have another 2 km to go to Western Lodge. (**Note:** This broad road provides fire access and maintenance route for the NCC. It leads to the fire tower atop the Luskville Falls. Originally, in the period of Parkway construction, this was supposed to be a paved extension to the park's western sector.)

Turn right on Ridge Road trail #1 and continue for approximately 700 metres until you find Western Trail, #9, heading through the woods on your left. Plunge into the cathedral-like quiet of the tall hardwood forests — watch for deer.

Soon you arrive at a major intersection where Western Trail crosses Ridge Road wooded trail #1B. (Confused? Yes, the gravelled Ridge Road is also called trail #1.) Turn right onto #1B where a sign says it is 4 km to Meech Lake. (See McCloskey walk.) Trail #1B wends its way through the woods, passing rock piles and then a large, old beaver pond. A small plantation of pine trees soon appears on your left.

Keep left, following McCloskey Trail, #2. Today an overgrown clearing marks part of the McCloskey family farm on your right. Remnants of a stone wall appear in the woods just past the clearing. The path descends through a hardwood forest with a number of rock

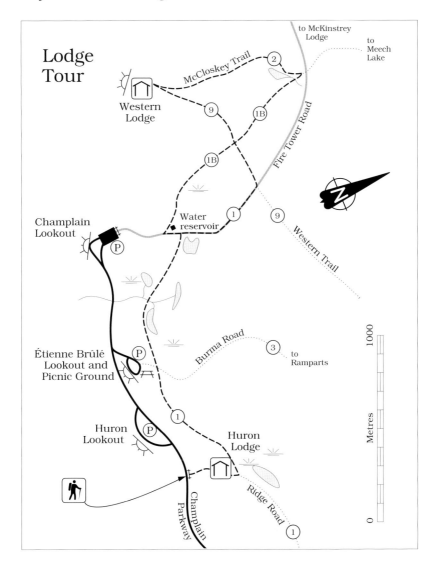

piles, unmistakable clues that the land was once cleared. After a short uphill grade beyond a creek, you descend to Western Lodge, with its beautiful view over the Ottawa River Valley.

From this vantage point, you can spy the Mountain Road veering off from the Eardley Escarpment to join Highway #148. In the lodge, an information panel informs you of the microclimate found here, and also of the winter deer-yards.

To return, retrace your steps up the hill and proceed right on narrow, rocky Western Trail, #9. Take this route to the major intersection with #1B that you met before. Now turn right. Follow this undulating trail over a small creek, past some wet spots until you see a 1940s water reservoir ahead to your left. A few more steps and you are back at the main Ridge Road, #1. Turn left up this gravelled trail for a few paces. Then rejoin your original route by veering right, into the woods on Ridge Road, #1, to Huron Lodge.

Intersecting trails: As mentioned.

Points of interest: Huron Lodge was built in the clearing left by the Grimes homestead, long since gone. The original chalet was built in 1964, providing a resting spot for cross-country skiers between Camp Fortune and Western Lodge. Although the Gatineau hills were predominantly the domain of Algonquin Indians, the Huron were known here. The lodge takes their name.

Western Lodge was originally built in East Templeton, being on the train route, but was moved to this location after the original Ottawa Ski Club Lodges became less dependent upon the railway. In 1945 it was torn down again and moved to Camp Fortune when downhill overtook cross-country skiing in popularity. Fortunately, Western Lodge was rebuilt here during the late sixties in a resurgence of enthusiasm for cross-country skiing.

Listen for the bird song and you may even catch a glimpse of a redstart, great eastern flycatcher, kingbird, or hermit thrush. During the summer I often see an indigo bunting on this hike, usually at the verge of woods in the McCloskey meadows.

Q: CHAMPLAIN LOOKOUT

NCC Interpreted Trail
1.2 km return
Allow .5 hour

This short, hilly trail features NCC signs along its route. It is of great geological interest, introducing you to a faulted ravine, and providing glimpses of marine and glacial influences of long ago.

Access: Take the Champlain Parkway turnoff from the Gatineau Parkway and go west to the Champlain Lookout. Park in the gravelled parking lot at the end of the Parkway loop.

Facilities: There are outhouses, garbage bins, NCC information panels, and trail brochures here.

Trail description: The trailhead is at the west (right) edge of the stone wall encircling the Champlain Lookout. It is a well-defined semi-circuit descending to an observation deck overlooking the Ottawa Valley. Beyond this you veer right and start a gentle climb, which returns you to the Champlain Lookout. (**Note:** because this trail is well-defined with NCC signs, I have not supplied a map.)

Enjoying the view west along the Eardley Escarpment at Champlain Lookout, September 2002. Photo: Katharine Fletcher.

Intersecting trails: None

Points of interest: The Champlain Lookout gives us insight into the effects of powerful geological forces on our environment. The broad Ottawa Valley plain is a rift valley extending into the United States; the Eardley Escarpment is its northern limit. A rift valley is created when earth slumps between major fault lines. One fault lies at the base of the ridge, along the Mountain Road; (another, more minor fault created the depression filled by the line of Philippe, Mousseau, and Meech lakes. The slumped valley floor is actually composed of younger rock than the ridge. Whereas the escarpment is Precambrian rock, notably gneiss, quartz and feldspar, the valley is primarily Ordovician rock, such as limestone.

The escarpment itself is ancient Canadian Shield rock, roots of the Laurentian Mountains that were once as high as the Rockies. After the rift valley was created approximately 270,000 years ago, the Wisconsin Ice Cap covered our part of North America for 30,000 years. This immense glacier was over 2 km high and receded only 12,000 years ago — rather a short time, geologically speaking. Glacial action further ground down the ridge to approximately its present height. The erosion continues today thanks to the well-known agents of wind, rain, snow, sleet, and ice, and the concurrent freezing, thawing, expansion, and contraction due to extremes of cold and heat, all exacerbated by the ridge's direct southerly exposure.

Notice the erratic on this trail. The giant boulder was once suspended in the glacier, having been ripped from its place of origin and dropped here.

The Ottawa Valley was once the bottom of the Champlain Sea. After the ice cap melted, the valley floor was depressed: water from what we know today as the Atlantic Ocean rushed in roughly 11,000 years ago. It is hard to believe that 200-metre deep salt waters lapped at the Eardley Escarpment, but if you visit the Museum of Nature in Ottawa you can see the fossils of marine creatures — including whales — that once swam here. Gradually the land rose after the weight of the ice lessened and the waters receded. Today, the modern-day watershed of the Ottawa River carves its path through the Valley.

The lookout may have derived its name from the sea. However, Champlain Lookout surveys the Ottawa River that explorer Samuel de Champlain paddled in 1613 in the company of Nicolas de Vignau and Native guides. They were searching for the elusive passage to the Pacific Ocean and Far East about which the English explorer Henry Hudson had written. Instead, the French expedition reached an Algonquin settlement at Allumette Island.

R: RIDGE ROAD 1 — OLD CHELSEA TO CHAMPLAIN LOOKOUT

Shared bike/hike trail; ski trail: #1

18 km return

Allow 8 hours

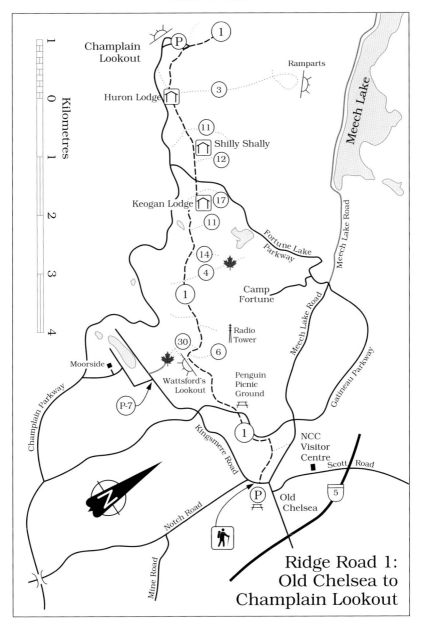

Ridge Road is the backbone of the Park. Because of its length, I split it into two hikes. In this first Ridge Road section, you go to several lookouts: Wattsford's, Étienne Brûlé, and Champlain, and three lodges: Keogan, Shilly Shally and Huron. **Hint:** Why not organize with friends? You could take two cars and leave one at either end of the hike.

Access: Turn left to Old Chelsea from Highway #5 turnoff. About 500 metres past the Scott Road intersection, take the left-hand turn onto Kingsmere Road. Almost immediately to your left is the Old Chelsea parking lot. Park here. **Note:** This lot is closed in winter. Alternatively you can park at the Visitor's Centre on Meech Lake Road or use P-7, Booth, on Kingsmere Road (see map).

Facilities: Outhouses, picnic tables, and barbecue pits.

Trail description: The trailhead is on the opposite side of Kingsmere Road. Ridge Road, #1, ascends through the woods. In 1.5 km you cross the Gatineau Parkway and walk beside the Penguin Picnic Ground. Continue for another 1.5 km and you soon arrive at Wattsford's Lookout, named after Colonel Wattsford, a member of the Ottawa Ski Club who had a home at Kingsmere Lake. Just beyond the lookout is the junction with Booth Trail, #30, and where #1 becomes part of the Trans-Canada Trail.

Proceed on Ridge Road past Skyline, #6. Follow the easy trail past a beaver pond and various intersections. In 1.5 km you get to where the Trans-Canada Trail leaves #1 at the junction with Fortune Lake, #4. This is the main trail leading to Camp Fortune. Stay on #1 and head along more hills until, after another 1.5 km, you reach Keogan Road, trail #17. Need a break? Head right to Keogan Lodge.

Otherwise, continue on soon crossing Fortune Lake Parkway. Just before you get to trail #12 you see Shilly Shally, the second lodge. It is about 1.7 km from here to Huron Lodge. En route you pass Long Merry-Go-Round, #11. Now you are 1.5 km from your destination, Champlain Lookout. Continue on #1 until you reach a gravel road, sometimes called the Fire Tower Road, which proceeds northwest to the top of Luskville Falls (see Luskville Falls walk). This gravel road is actually Ridge Road, #1.

Turn left at this gravel road. After a few paces you see a gate. Pass by the gate, through the parking lot on the other side, and proceed to the stone wall of the Champlain Lookout.

To return to your car, retrace your steps.

Intersecting trails: As I've mentioned above, many trails intersect with #1. Several form circuits or interesting diversions of their own, so check out the NCC trails map.

Points of interest: The names of the intersecting trails have their own story, for they were carved out of the bush by either the Night or Trail Riders, the trail-builders of the Ottawa Ski Club. Here's how Penguin Picnic Ground got its name:

> … one cold winter day just as the sun was sinking, a gang of Night Riders led by Captain Joe Morin was busy putting the finishing touches on the new trail and snipping the last barbed wire when they heard a noise like the flapping of wings in a deep ravine near by. Joe went over to investigate and found a rather large, strange-looking bird floundering helplessly in the snow. He picked it up tenderly, put it in his haversack, and brought it to the dormitory of Camp Fortune Lodge where the bird quickly revived under the influence of warmth and good food. It was at once identified as a penguin by C.E. Mortureux who had seen a few penguins in zoos, and pictures of them in books and had read a lot about their habits. The bird stood up exactly like a penguin, making a neat little bow whenever anyone entered the dormitory, uttering an incessant prattle that no one could understand, not even the Night Riders, accustomed though they were to the meaning of strange sounds in the bush.[74]

This tongue-in-cheek story ends with the admission that the bird was most probably a razor-billed auk, "close relative of the penguin, known under the name of *Pingouin commune*." Of course, "Penguin" suited a trail and picnic ground better than "razor-billed auk." And thus the name was born. (It makes a good story, but the "auk" was probably a thick-billed murre.)

Local legends claim that Ridge Road was once an Algonquin footpath, an escape route from the busier waterways of the Gatineau and Ottawa rivers which were populated by their Native and French competitors. In the early 1800s, it was widened into a road by settlers such as Dunlop and McCloskey, who required access to their homesteads. In the 1900s, private access blossomed into the development of the network of trails for cross-country and downhill skiers. By the 1940s a system of fire access routes was imperative, and Ridge Road provided an arterial route.

S: RIDGE ROAD 2 — CHAMPLAIN LOOKOUT TO FIRE TOWER

Shared hike/bike and ski trail: #1
23 km return (to fire tower)
Allow 10 hours

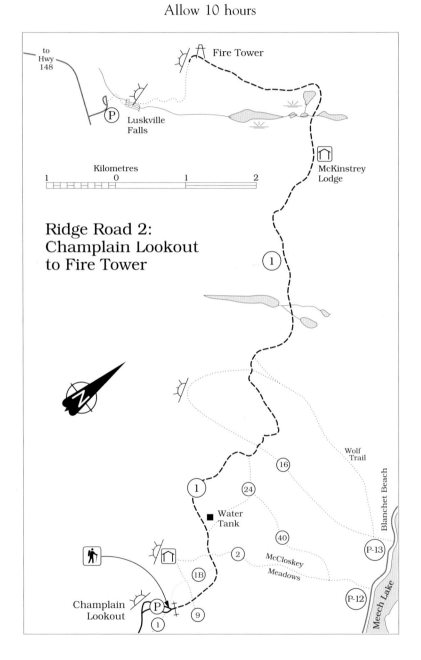

to
Hwy
148

Fire Tower

P Luskville
Falls

McKinstrey
Lodge

Kilometres

Ridge Road 2:
Champlain Lookout
to Fire Tower

Wolf
Trail

Blanchet Beach

16

1   24

Water
Tank

40

P-13

2   McCloskey
Meadows

1B

P-12

Champlain
Lookout   P

9

1

Meech Lake

This most westerly section of Ridge Road, from Champlain Lookout to the base of Luskville Falls, via Western and McKinstrey Lodges and the Fire Tower, is the most challenging trail of the book in terms of both distance and terrain. It is a gorgeous walk, taking you through beech "bear tree" woods and beside active beaver ponds. **Hint:** This is a long hike; consider organizing two cars and leave one at either end of the hike to reduce the distance and time.

Access: Turn left (west) onto the Champlain Parkway from the Gatineau Parkway and continue until you reach the Champlain Lookout. The main parking lot of the Champlain Lookout is to your right. Park here.

Facilities: Garbage bins, NCC interpretive signs at Champlain Lookout. Outhouses here and at Western Lodge.

Trail description: Head to the northern end of the parking lot where there is a gate restricting vehicle access to Ridge Road. Stay on the gravel, wide road (sometimes called Fire Tower Road) for almost 1.5 km you will intersect with McCloskey Trail, #2. (If you want to take a diversion to Western Lodge head left on #2 [see McCloskey walk]. The lodge offers a dramatic view over the Eardley Escarpment to the Ottawa Valley and Mountain Road. Retrace your steps to reconnect to #1.)

Continue on #1. Soon you pass #24, heading north (right). At this junction there is a water tank: a reminder of old fire prevention strategies. Stay on Ridge Road. You pass #16 to Meech Lake, the last well-defined trail you will see for some time.

You now enter a less-travelled section of the park. For the next 6 km to McKinstrey Lodge you walk up and down hilly terrain, beside active beaver ponds and smooth-barked beech trees. Some of these are dramatically marked by bear claws. The trail passes beside several beaver pond meadows — look for white-tailed deer. Once at McKinstrey Lodge, you may wish to take a well earned break.

Proceed on #1 which soon veers left. The next kilometre or so becomes progressively higher and drier. Precambrian rock is exposed to view and pine trees whisper in the wind. Ahead, in an open area, is the old fire tower — now adorned with solar panels, a wind turbine on the top, and a security camera.

This may be the extent of your trek. If so, return to the Champlain Lookout the way you came. However, you can descend the 2.2 km rocky trail to the base of Luskville Falls. (Remember: it takes twice as long to clamber back up, so judge your time and energy accordingly, unless you are being picked up at Luskville Falls Picnic Ground.)

If you make it to the bottom, you have walked a total of roughly 12.2 km — one way — from Champlain Lookout.

The Fire Tower, 1985. Photo: Laurie Schell.

Intersecting trails: Many intersections mark Ridge Road. Some can be taken to alternative destinations. You may wish to pre-arrange having a friend pick you up at some of these places, for return routes are long.

#2, #24, then #40: to the northeast these trails descend to Meech Lake.

#16 Wolf Trail: to lookouts over the Ottawa Valley.

Old #10: passes Lakes Charette and Gauthier, descending sharply to Lusk Cave and to Lac Philippe, a distance of 4.5 km.

Points of interest: There is a lot to see and explore along this more remote section of the park. The beech "bear trees" are of special note.

Beaver ponds are always fascinating. Be as quiet as possible and you may be rewarded by seeing a beaver even during the midday heat. Watch for one swimming about in the pond: look for its wake cutting the water's surface. Listen for the munching sound, made as it nibbles on juicy shoots and leaves ...

T: LUSKVILLE FALLS

Hiking trail
NCC interpreted trail
5 km return to fire tower
Allow 2.5–3 hours

This is a very steep, rocky scramble that criss-crosses the falls along the Eardley Escarpment. It rewards you with breathtaking views of the Upper Ottawa Valley, west to Pontiac County. Wear sturdy shoes with a gripping sole for this strenuous uphill climb.

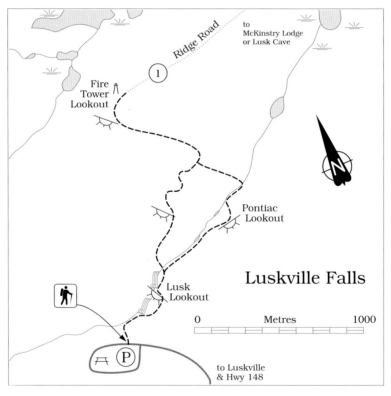

Access: This hike requires more planning as it takes forty minutes to drive to the falls from downtown Ottawa. Head west on Highway #148 through Aylmer, or take the Mountain Road and turn right onto #148. On your right, in the midst of the four-lane highway at Luskville, you will notice the Luskville Town Hall and a Gatineau Park sign on your right. Turn right on Hotel de Ville Street and proceed down the gravel road for .5 km. Turn left at the sign to the picnic ground or, if the barrier is closed — as in early spring — park on side of the road. **Note:** There is a riding stable at the foot of the falls, on your right, where you can rent a horse. This is the only stable, to date, which offers authorized rides along selected routes in Gatineau Park.

Facilities: Outhouses, picnic tables, barbecue sites, and garbage bins. Horseback riding.

Trail description: The trailhead starts at steps descending to a footbridge over a stream, then up a gentle ascent to the base of the waterfall. Here there is a sign pointing 200 metres to Lusk Lookout. The path veers away from the falls and ascends alongside a sheer cliff face. At the top, follow the NCC blue hiking signs pointing left to Lusk Lookout at the top of the first falls. Take a break here to admire the view over the flat Ottawa Valley floor.

To proceed to the next lookout, ascend the rocks to the top of the next falls. There is a crossing here which you will use on your descent, but for now, stay on the east side of the creek. The trail follows the creek, then diverges right to ascend more exposed rock to Pontiac Lookout. Pause again: from here you can get a panorama of the valley. For instance, across from you on the south side of the Ottawa River is Constance Bay. To your right (west) is the Pontiac region. This

A challenging uphill hike can be accomplished by all ages. My nephew Patrick climbing the rocks at Luskville Falls. Photo: Eric Fletcher, November 1984.

sprawling, visually stunning area extends as far as you can see, north and west of the Ottawa River past Luskville, Shawville, and Fort Coulonge to Sheenboro and beyond. On a clear day you can spot the spires of the Catholic Church in Quyon, upriver.

At this point, another sign points 1 km to the Fire Tower and you'll note you have already climbed 1.5 km. The trail now descends back to the creek, then follows alongside to a birch grove where you find a crossing place. Cross the stream and continue uphill through more exposed Precambrian rock and pine trees. Note the fork in the trail. For now, proceed straight uphill to the fire tower.

You emerge from the woods into a cleared area with the fire tower straight ahead. All the old fire warden's buildings have been demolished. You'll note a bank of solar panels at the base of the tower, a wind turbine at the top — and a security camera mounted inside the fenced area. To your right is the westernmost end of Ridge Road, #1.

To return, you can retrace your steps entirely, or turn right at the first fork. It takes you down via a series of rocky scrambles and crosses the creek above the second falls. Exercise caution as you descend through the stunted oak trees: their leaves are extremely slippery on the rock.

Intersecting trails:

#1 Ridge Road: At the summit, trail #1 heads right (east) to McKinstrey Lodge, roughly 3 km from the base of the tower and an 11 km return hike from the base of the falls. Many fishermen follow the lure of trout and go to Charette and Gauthier lakes. Of course, you could take Ridge Road all the way to Old Chelsea, a full day's walk or several hours by bicycle.

Points of interest: The Eardley Escarpment provides a superb vantage point from which to view the Ottawa Valley. Imagine the fur traders and explorers canoeing upriver accompanied by native guides. Perhaps Étienne Brûlé paddled by in 1610, and you can read Samuel de Champlain's daily journal of his travels here in 1613. Later on, steamships plied these waters, from Aylmer to Quyon, and beyond, up into the Pontiac.

The fire tower stands in testimony to the many fires that have raged over the hills in the past. Both it and the shelter structures were probably erected during the 1930s and '40s. You can still see blackened stumps as you climb the escarpment.

The change in vegetation is dramatic, from delicate spring beauties and wild ginger on the forest floor at the base of the falls, to stunted white and red oak that are over a hundred years old. These trees are stunted because of the scant topsoil and exposure. The NCC signs explain that vegetation here is similar to that found 200 km to the north.

U: PINE ROAD TO HERRIDGE LODGE

Shared bike/hike & ski trail #50
1 km return
Allow 1.5 hour

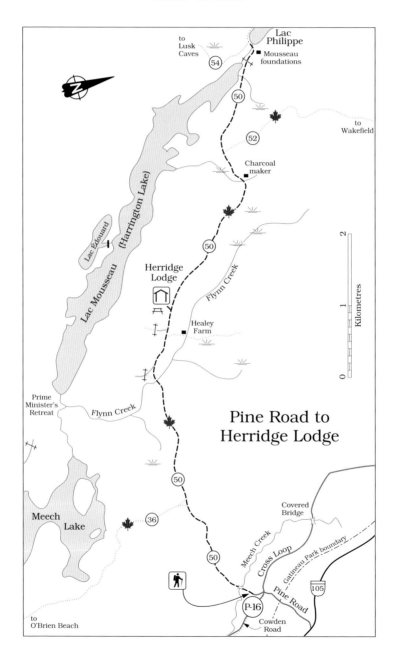

It's a pleasure to include this trail: Since 1994 the Meech Creek Valley has belonged to Gatineau Park. Pine Road (Meech Creek) parking lot is now open year-round for hikers, bikers, and skiers. There's history galore up in these hills, so lace up your boots and we're off.

Access: Take Highway #5 north and drive to its termination. Turn left on Highway 105 to drive north towards Wakefield. Turn left on Pine Road and drive .8 km to its end: park at Meech Valley lot P-16.

Facilities: An outhouse at the lot; at Herridge there is a cozy wood stove, outhouses, and picnic tables inside and outside the lodge; wild bird feeder.

The old Healey homestead with exposed rocks showing in the fields, n.d. NCC historical files H14–565.

Trail description: Find the trailhead at the west corner of the lot. It points you 5 km to Herridge Lodge via ski trail #50. Walk up the old Foxfarm Road — the "Pine Road trail," a wide roadbed that eventually goes to Lac Mousseau (Harrington Lake) and the old Healey Farm. A gurgling creek carves its way through mossy banks on your right. Continue along this trail for about 2 km. (A signpost points you southeast on #36, Discovery Trail, leading to O'Brien Beach.) Stay on trail #50.

The original circa 1840 settlers' fields have all but disappeared; open spaces are overgrown with pine, spruce and birch trees. You are now entering the old property of Cameron Edwards, who had his fox farm here. He and Herridge owned almost 4,000 acres which they sold to the FDC (precursor of NCC) in 1951. Continue up this hilly terrain. You cross Flynn Creek. Soon a gate bars your exploration of a lane leading left. This was the old roadway to the prime minister's summer retreat.

Herridge Lodge, the former Cafferty homestead, 1975. The stone pillars and home were restored by the NCC. From NCC file H14–365.

Stay on the main trail as it veers right, uphill. To your left is a 250-metre knoll. After about 700 metres a trail leads right to the old Healey farm: Stan and Dorothy left it in 1955. Explore if you wish, then return to #50. Continue roughly 100 metres and on your left, between fieldstone pillars, is another gate barring a path leading to the former summer cottage of William Herridge, which became the prime minister's guest cottage after the 1959 sale. Proceed on #50 another .5 km to Herridge Lodge, to your left. Pause here.

Contine on trail #50, heading left up the broad roadway. After roughly 2.5 km the path veers left. At the "corner," look right, into the woods. Can you find the 1930's charcoal maker? After another 500 metres, you will pass by trail #52, the extension of the Trans-

Canada Trail leading to Wakefield and parking lot P-17. Stay on #50: you soon pass another 250-metre knoll on your left.

Now continue approximately 1.5 km. Walk just beyond the gate. About 200 metres beyond it, look for the foundations to the Mousseau homestead, after whom Lac Mousseau is named. On the left side of #50 find their root cellar; on the right the old building foundation. The gates are of note because they were built by the FDC in 1951 to keep the public away from the prime ministerial grounds.

The covered bridge over Meech Creek on the "Cross Loop Road" near Pine Road, August 2002. Photo: Katharine Fletcher.

Turn around and retrace your steps back to your car.

Intersecting trails:

#36 Discovery Trail: (here part of the Trans-Canada Trail) heads south towards Meech Lake and O'Brien Beach.

#52: Here part of the Trans-Canada Trail heads almost due north near the charcoal burner. It connects to Wakefield and parking lot P-17. **Suggestion:** Take two cars; park one at both parking lots (P-16 and P-17) and create a different circuit if you walk with friends.

Points of interest: What is known today as Pine Road, trail #50, used to be Foxfarm Road, after Colonel Edward's venture. But long before Edward's time, both it and the Mousseau Road were settlement roads, farmed by families like Daly, Cross, Dean, Finnerty, Cafferty, and Flynn. Hendricks had a farm near Cafferty's (Herridge Lodge) and used to haul wood to heat the parliament buildings, bringing it out of the forest by oxen-drawn cart. Indeed, there was a bustling community in these parts, complete with "Healey's [or Flynn's] School," a log building once located on the Mousseau Road (trail #50) past Healey's farm. Families made money as they could and tales abound: Harry Flynn took a "quarter of a million dollars worth of mica from the hillside north of Cafferty's house: worth $100 a ton. Sometimes took out as much as 7 tons a day."[75] Still others, like the Proulx family, gathered and sold a wild plant, perhaps ginseng.[76]

Herridge Lodge was the Cafferty home, a square-timber structure. Here's what J. Cafferty recalled: "I was born in the 'old' house, which was on the east side of the road. Nothing left of it now. Ambrose, the baby, was 2 years old when we moved into the 'new' house [Herridge Lodge]. That would make it 72 years old [in 1966] … Christie Allen and Tom McAdam finished the house. The Frenchmen made the shingles — split blocks fine enough for shingles."[77]

The barn opposite P-16 was built by Wyman Cross in 1916.

V: BROWN LAKE & WAKEFIELD MILL

Shared hike/bike/ski trail #53 & #52;
unnumbered loop
4 km return (with mill)
Allow 2.5 hours

This trail takes you to Brown Lake and then, if you wish, you can cross over to the Wakefield Mill on a new connecting trail that's not for bikes. Why not explore the village of Wakefield before returning to your car? **Note:** Wakefield Mill is an auberge/inn. Also, you can register for an overnight stay at Brown Lake cabin (but you must call the Visitor's Centre to reserve it).

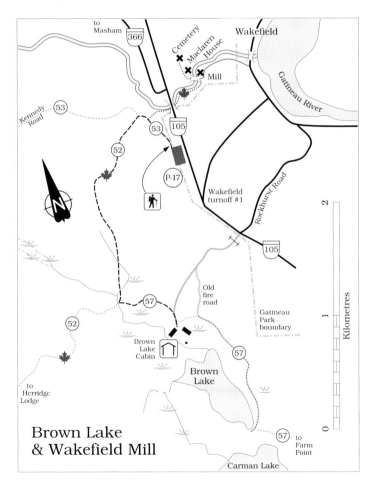

Brown Lake & Wakefield Mill

Access: Take Highway #5 north from Hull to its termination at Highway #105. Turn left at the lights. Continue another 8 km to P-17 which appears on your left, after you have passed the first turnoff to Wakefield. If you get to the left-hand turn to Highway #366 to Masham, you've gone too far.

Facilities: At P-17: outhouse; at Brown Lake: outhouses, picnic tables, garbage bins, wild bird feeder; at Wakefield Mill: NCC interpretive signs. Brown Cabin can be booked for an overnight experience by reservation only; call the Visitor's Centre.

Trail description: Find the trailhead at the northwest corner of P-17. This is Kennedy Road, trail #53 (see Kennedy Road walk). It crosses the open fields for 300 metres and comes to a sign and another trail leading 1 km right, to the Wakefield Mill.

Brown Lake Cabin. NCC Gatineau Park slide collection.

For now, continue on #53 for another 500 metres past a little gully to your right. Another sign appears. Now turn left on trail #52 rising through the woods to Brown Lake and Chalet, 3 km. away. (**Note:** you can get to Herridge Lodge on #52, too — a 9.5 km walk — see

Pine Road walk.) You ascend through mixed hardwoods. On your left is an open field. Be sure to carry binoculars because the verges between habitats (wood and field, for example) are rich with wildlife. You may see a northern harrier gliding just above the fields, or a red-tail hawk soaring overhead. Continue along the gentle, hilly terrain. After 2.4 km you reach another signpost; turn sharply left (Herridge Lodge is another 7.5 km away).

Immediately after you veer left you cross a wet spot. Continue and you connect with a very pretty, wide old roadbed, winding around the edge of a hill. Very shortly you catch a glimpse of Brown Lake and Chalet. There's a marshy spot to explore: here there are many alder trees. Also, look for beaver and muskrat there, behind the chalet. To return to P-17, retrace your steps.

Intersecting trails:

Wakefield Mill, Maclaren House, and cemetery: Starting from P-17, turn right at the first fork described above (at the 300 metre mark).

Maclaren House, Wakefield, circa 1900. Collection of Dr. Stuart and Norma Geggie. NAC C–64877.

After 800 metres the path emerges just west of Highway #5, where the Lapêche River flows underneath first the old bridge, then the new one. Cross beneath the bridge; it's another 400 metres to the mill. You hug the side of the Lapêche River before it becomes the mill race. Ahead of you is the gristmill; to your left, across the bridge spanning the river is a white frame house — the miller's house; and on your right is Maclaren House. This broad path is actually the Kennedy Road extension (see Kennedy Road walk) which connected that community to the mill and village.

To get to the cemetery, walk up the road leading uphill behind Maclaren House. The Canadian flag flying atop a tall flagpole marks the cemetery. The 1870 grave of David Maclaren is here; and in the northeast corner find the grave of former Prime Minister Lester B. Pearson.

The Maclaren House in April 2002.
Photo: Katharine Fletcher.

The Wakefield Mill, now an inn, April 2002.
Photo: Katharine Fletcher.

#52 to #50: #52 connects to #50 and Herridge Lodge. Going right (west) on #50 gets you to Lac Philippe; you could do a circuit to P-17 via #51 and Kennedy Road, #53. Trails #52 and #50 connect with #36, all being part of the shared Trans-Canada Trail system. You could bike all the way to Old Chelsea, Hull, or even head to the fire tower atop Luskville Falls.

Points of interest: Brown Lake and Chalet are named for the family who settled here. Black Luke's farm was at the intersection of trail #50 (once called Nichol's Road) and the turnoff to Brown Lake. The Browns were a large family and some sported colourful names: Jimmy in the Natch Brown and Natch-Henry Brown and Charlie Brown lived around Brown Lake. Black Luke's Road was the name of the trail you take to Brown Lake; at one time there were "20 teams of horses drawn out this road, from Mousseau out to Brown Lake."[78]

Wakefield grist mill. The first was built in 1838 by William Fairbairn, a Scottish immigrant who immediately recognized the market for flour among the early settlers. David Maclaren and his sons, James and John, bought it in 1844 and expanded it into a complex, complete with sawmill (on the opposite side of the Lapêche), woollen and carding mills. Over time, a succession of fires swept the complex; the grist mill is the only survivor. It is now a privately operated auberge/inn with a restaurant open to the public.

Maclaren House. This Victorian gothic, variegated brick home was built sometime in the 1860s and was home to John and possibly James Maclaren, before the latter left for Buckingham. In 1960 it was sold to the NCC. The Victorian gothic home has had a varied life as private home, Lapêche library, and a local museum. Today it is part of the Wakefield Mill Inn.

Maclaren Cemetery. The late author/historian Pat Evans noted that the earliest date of death is on Jane Townsend's 1868 tombstone. Evans also observed that the highest (and ergo most preferable) ground is occupied by the Townsend family. Here, too, rest many Maclarens, including David.

W: KENNEDY ROAD

Ski trails: #50 & #51
Full circuit is 14.5 km
Allow 4 hours

This easy trail leads through land once farmed by the Kennedy family. Dalton Kennedy sold his farm to the NCC in 1947. It traverses a variety of zones — marsh, meadow, hardwood, and evergreen woods, and is often wet along the first part of the trail: wear appropriate shoes.

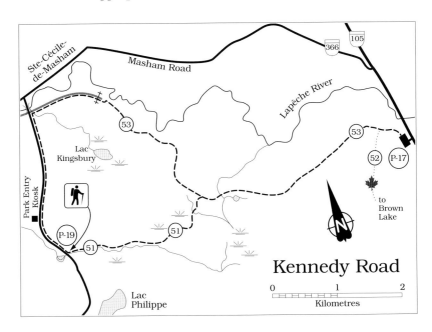

Access: Take Highway #105 from Hull and go north towards Wakefield, past the towns of Kirk's Ferry and Farm Point. At the junction, turn left onto Highway #366, and drive about 8 km until you arrive at Ste-Cécile-de-Masham. Turn left at the Lac Philippe sign into Gatineau Park, and cross through the covered bridge. Immediately after the bridge there is a road. (Don't turn here but make a mental note, for this is where you'll emerge from your hike during summer.) You pass by a park kiosk and self-serve information centre where you'll probably pay a fee during summer. Keep on driving and P-19 appears on your left. Park here. **Note:** At time of writing, in early 2004, the use of trail #53 is a contentious issue. Summer ATV users make it difficult for hikers. Snowmobilers use the trail in winter, and Quebec prohibits hiking or skiing on snowmobile trails. In short, take caution on this trail.

Facilities: Outhouse, garbage bins. **Tip:** take a wide-brimmed hat because the sunshine can be hot in the fields.

Trail description: At P-19, find the trailhead to #51 heading to your right (east) through a pine plantation. Almost immediately there is a wet area for about 500 metres and the hill to your left is predominantly hardwood. After 1 km you pass a small lake on your right just before you reach a fork in the trail.

Turn right on Kennedy Road, #53. You now walk its length, a distance of 4 km to the Wakefield P-17. You pass through mixed softwoods such as hemlock, balsam, and spruce that graduate into hardwoods before becoming open meadowland. At the pastureland, look for lilacs on either side of the path indicating old homestead sites. As well, former property fence lines can be deduced in the lines of trees, some of which shelter crumbling rock walls. You may also be able to find some old wire fencing, deeply embedded in still-growing tree "posts." Continue down this easy road, skirting the Lapêche River on your left. 300 metres beyond the intersection with the Trans-Canada Trail, #52, you reach P-17 and Highway #366. Retrace your steps to your car.

Or, do a longer circuit by continuing on trail #53 which veers to the right at the very first fork that you came to after heading out (see map): it is a 6.5 km loop back towards Lac Philippe and your car at P-19. This is a very pretty part of Kennedy Road. It follows the meandering Lapêche River, now on your right, and you can explore the river bank. The roadbed hugs the north-facing ridge on the left. In late November of '96 there was a "highway" of animal prints leading across the trail to the open water of the Lapêche. It is a great spot for track identification. In the distance through the pastures to your right, you catch glimpses of Highway #366 and then the farmhouses near the village of Ste-Cécile-de-Masham. Ahead of you, after a hike of about 2.5 km past the fork, you see a barrier gate. In winter, ski trail #53 will take you left, through a farmer's field, to P-19. But in summer, when the fields are in use, do not use this section of #53 since you'll damage the crop. Instead, walk around the gate. Proceed on the road: soon you will see the small covered bridge over the Lapêche River which you drove through earlier. Turn left at the paved Lac Philippe Road and walk on the grassy shoulder back to P-19, almost 3 km. Keep a lookout after you pass the culvert and stream: you can rejoin #53 on your left as it angles up, through the woods, walking perhaps 250 metres to your car.

Intersecting trails:

#52: towards the end of #53, in sight of the barrier to Highway #366, another old road angles sharply to the right, almost due south; it goes to Brown Lake (see Brown Lake walk). Eventually, it joins trail #50 to Herridge Lodge. Examine the NCC trail maps because from here, you can connect to O'Brien Beach via the Discovery trail (#50) and #36.

Points of interest: There used to be a sizable settlement along what was the Lapêche Creek Road, sometimes called the Trowse Settlement Road. Names of families that lived by what is now trail #53 included Charlie Kingsbury (after whom the lake is named), Hod Trowse, and Billy Otterson, whose daughter married Dalton Kennedy; others were Dougherty, McNair, McCorkell, and Biron. With the exception of Art Biron who was French-Canadian, most settlers were English. At the intersection of trail #52 was George Trowse's home and the families of Duncan, Thomas, and Luke Brown. Joining trail #52 was Black Luke's Road leading to Brown's Lake, one of the more popular swimming holes of the area. Now open meadowland lies where land was once farmed and homesteads built.

The walk takes you through good bird watching terrain. Watch for the kestrel (sparrow hawk), northern harrier, and red-tailed hawk skimming above the fields in search of their prey. In the woods listen for the rat-a-tat-tat of the downy, hairy, or pileated woodpeckers, and for the drumming of the ruffed grouse. In the meadows watch for the meadowlark with its speckled, yellow breast, and the bobbing flight of the black, gold, and white bobolink.

In the flooded wetlands of Lapêche Creek you may be lucky and see a beaver or muskrat. Observe the beaver's efforts at dam building as you walk along the first wet area on trail #51. Look for flattened vegetation at the water's edge, indicating where he dragged his latest tree, and see if you can spot paw prints in the mud. Imagine how much energy it must take the beaver to haul a tree many times his own size through the undergrowth to the water.

At the verge of forest and meadow, keep your eyes peeled for a white-tailed deer. They like to browse at the forest edge where they can dart quickly into the safety of the woods. On my first hike here, I spotted a stag with two does. If you see one, notice how quickly it catches your scent, and how it melts into the forest …

X: LUSK CAVE

Hike/ski trail: #50, #54
12 km full circuit
Allow 3–5 hours

Does cave exploration catch your fancy? This is a beautiful walk taking you through a hilly, wooded trail to a point of geological interest: the Lusk Cave. The cave can be entered. Be sure to take a flashlight and sturdy shoes if you intend to explore it. **Note:** At time of writing, parts of this trail are shared bike/hike: please check with the NCC.

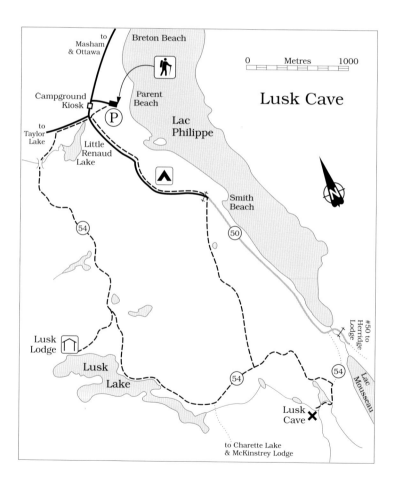

Access: Take Highway #105 from Hull and go north past the second exit to Wakefield. At the junction with Highway #366, turn left and drive about 8 km until you arrive at Ste-Cécile-de-Masham. Turn left at the Lac Philippe sign into Gatineau Park, cross through the 1958 covered bridge and park at Parent Beach. **Note:** in winter, you must park at P-19 (see Kennedy Road walk map) and ski in; on trail #50, where there is a fee in summer.

Facilities: Lac Philippe and its accompanying campground, Taylor Lake, is one of the best-equipped areas of the Park: 280 overnight camping sites are available with five sites for group camping. In season, there are first aid and food kiosks, an information kiosk, swimming, picnic, and barbecue areas, changing rooms, boat and canoe rentals. It is one of the few areas in the park that has public pay telephones. During winter, a system of hut-to-hut trails and overnight lodging is available here for a fee. Reserve early: they fill fast. Do you want to explore the cave? Take clothes you don't mind getting wet: water inside the cave can be knee-high. Bring an extra pair of shoes.

Trail description: The trailhead to the Lusk Cave trail, #50, is at Parent Beach parking lot. Follow the signs along trail #50. The trail continues to a pole gate and then immediately leaves the roadbed, heading right, up through the mixed hardwoods. The woodland trail is hilly; you pass a beaver pond on your left and continue climbing until you reach trail #54. Turn left, proceed almost a kilometre to the cave. The trail curves around a beaver pond: look for tadpoles and snapping turtles here. Another fork in the trail appears: stay right to ascend even hillier terrain, to the caves. NCC interpretive signs await you there.

To return, retrace your steps back to Parent Beach.

Circuit: You may wish to do the 12 km circuit walk to Lusk Lake and Lodge. Return .5 km to the first fork and bear left on #54. Continue on this path, and pass the second fork (the trail you ascended earlier, #50). After about 1 km another trail (old #10 that goes up to Lac Charette, McKinstrey Lodge, and Ridge Road) appears to your left. Continue past this turnoff, staying on trail #54 for another 1.5 km until you reach a gravel road. En route you pass wonderful rock lookouts over Lusk Lake, where I saw my first loon babies perched on their mother's back while she swam about. Turn left at the roadbed to walk the 700 metres to Lusk Lodge. To return to Parent Beach, head back down the road. Just past the intersection marking the path to Lusk

Cave, there is a large beaver meadow on your right. Look out for white-tailed deer here.

You emerge at the Taylor Lake Road after about a 2 km gradual descent through balsam woods. It is a glorious ski in winter when these evergreens are laden with snow. Keep right until you see the park campground kiosk. Head left towards it. Then take the right-hand fork in the road. Follow the signs to Parent Beach. You will leave the pavement to rejoin a sandy road for a few metres. You soon see Parent Beach and your car. In summer, it's heavenly to go for a swim after this long circuit.

Intersecting trails:

#50: (Please see the NCC ski/summer trails map.) You can go to Herridge Lodge via #50, and from there loop to O'Brien Beach's P-11, or else go to Kennedy Road. Truly lots of options.

West from Taylor Lake: There is a great lookout which overlooks the top of the escarpment (see NCC trail maps). This road was supposed to be the extension of the western parkway but it was never built. It would have traversed Ridge Road west, past the fire tower to connect here, west of Taylor Lake.

Points of interest: Named after a pioneer family, the Lusk Cave is intriguing and easily explored. Although caves are considered rare in the hard rock of the Canadian Shield, here in the Gatineau Valley a few are found, notably the Laflêche Cave on the east side of the Gatineau River.

The Lusk Cave was formed over 12,500 years ago, first by glacial meltwater carving its way into cracks in the rock. The water started to erode these cracks until underground tunnels eventually appeared. About 11,000 years ago the meltwater rush was over. A period of more gradual erosion started — erosion continued today by Lusk Creek.

Look for animal tracks in the sand along trail #50 and also along the beaches of Lac Philippe. You may see cloven hoof prints left by the white-tailed deer as they come down from the woods to drink, or be able to identify the imprint of porcupine and raccoon along the beach. Telltale piles of clam shells in the shallow waters of the lake are usually a hint that a raccoon has been by for an evening feed. Listen for the haunting cry of the loon at either Lusk or Philippe lakes, one of the loveliest calls of the wild.

⊠ Acknowledgements

Since 1985 when I first dreamed of *Historical Walks*, I have enjoyed substantial support from so many of you — my readers, my "students" with whom I have hiked, friends and family — that is impossible to name everyone. However, some of you have made oustanding contributions over the years, and it is these people and organizations I particulary want to mention.

First I thank my dear husband Eric, who is my life partner, outdoor companion, map-maker and business partner.

Some of the staff at the National Capital Commission have assisted Eric with maps and me with many other details over the years: these include Park Director Jean-René Doyon, Michel Viens, François Leduc, and Daniel Blais.

Historical Walks has introduced me to many kindred spirits and cemented ties with others. Elspeth Butterworth's poetry readings during hike lunch breaks and her delight in nature inspire me. Laurie Schell, my sister-in-law, shares my thrill at the success of *Historical Walks*; Laurie walked every hike and researched every map for the first edition and continues to spur me on to great adventures. I also greatly appreciate assistance from friend and neighbour, Chuck Lalonde, who worked with me to create the translations of all the French quotations.

Members of the Gatineau Valley Historical Society (formerly the Historical Society of the Gatineau until spring 2003) have provided constant support, encouragement, and information over the years. In particular I want to thank the Society's archivist Jay Atherton for his unwavering enthusiasm. Thanks, also, to the Society's digital database archivist Adrienne Herron, who who tells me she has enjoyed all the walks in this book, and who gains the same enjoyment from the park and its human and natural history as I do. I have also greatly benefited from innumerable members who contributed valuable essays and photographs to the Society's annual publication, *Up the Gatineau!* Thanks, each and every one of you: your information and stories are vital.

I want to thank the team at Fitzhenry & Whiteside, particularly production coordinator Marie Peters, for publishing *Historical Walks*, which has hitherto been self-published by me. It was a difficult decision to relinquish control... but I am delighted with the look and feel of this new third edition. Fitzhenry & Whiteside are publishing two other volumes in my series of historical guides to Canada's capital region: *Capital Walks: Walking Tours of Ottawa* (2nd edition) and, in spring 2004, my new book *Capital Rambles: Exploring the National Capital Region*.

Lastly, a huge thanks to my dear friend, my eighty-eight-year-old mother. It is she who encouraged my exploration of the natural world while I was a young girl growing up in Alderley Edge, England. Mum, thanks for teaching me to love and honour the ways of the wild: your legacy and influence continues.

Katharine Fletcher
January, 2004

> P.S. Special Notes to My Readers: For readability, bibliographic references have been gathered as Endnotes in the final pages. I have used the following abbreviations in the text: some photographs bear the acronym "NAC" for the National Archives of Canada; and "n.d." means "not dated." Similarly, "NCC" is National Capital Commission; "FDC" is Federal District Commission.

> Finally: while I strive for accuracy, in both historical or details and trail descriptions, new facts come to light, and trail signage (and even the routes of paths) can change over time. I invite you to contact me with your comments on the history, trails, and maps in this new edition. Thank you for your help. Please contact me with your thoughts and comments. Katharine Fletcher, 4316 Steele Line, Quyon, Québec J0X 2V0 e-mail: chesley@allstream.net

⬚ Selected Bibliography

Here is a brief list of some of my favourite local references. (Note: I have not included the Audubon, Stokes or Peterson Field guides; nor NCC reports or Master Plans as they are so numerous.) HSG refers to the Historical Society of the Gatineau (now Gatineau Valley Historical Society).

Aldred, Diane. *The Aylmer Road: An Illustrated History*. Aylmer, Quebec: Aylmer Heritage Association, 1994.

Andrews, J. David. *Gatineau Park: An Intimate Portrait*. Ottawa: Dynamic Light, 1994.

Baird, David M. *Guide to the Geology and Scenery of the National Capital Area*. Ottawa: Queen's Printer, 1968.

Brunton, Daniel F. *Nature and Natural Areas in Canada's Capital*. Ottawa: The Ottawa Citizen and The Ottawa Field-Naturalists' Club, 1988.

Champlain, Samuel de. *The Voyages and Explorations of Samuel de Champlain (1604–1616)* narrated by himself, Volume II, Translated by Annie Nettleton Bourne. Toronto: Courier Press, 1911.

Evans, Patrick M.O. *A Tale of Two Chelseas, Quebec*. Ottawa: Les Éditions J. Oscar Lemieux, 1988.

Fletcher, Katharine. *Capital Walks: Walking Tours of Ottawa*. Markham: Fitzhenry & Whiteside, 2004.

Gard, Anson A. *Pioneers of the Upper Ottawa, Humors of the Valley* and *Genealogy of the Valley*. Ottawa: Emerson, 1906.

Geggie, Norma and Stuart. *Lapêche: A History of the Townships of Wakefield and Masham in the Province of Quebec 1792 to 1925*. Old Chelsea, Quebec: HSG, 1980.

Geggie, Norma. *Wakefield and Its People: Tours of the Village*. Quyon, Quebec: Chesley House Publications, 1990.

Hessel, Peter. *The Algonkin Tribe*. Arnprior, Ont.: Kichesippi Books, 1987.

Hogarth, Donald. *Pioneer Mines of the Gatineau Region, Quebec*. Ottawa: University of Ottawa, 1975.

Hughson, John W. and Courtney C. J. Bond. *Hurling Down the Pine*. Old Chelsea, Quebec: HSG, 1964.

Le Nord de L'Outaouais: Manuel-Répertoire d'Histoire et de Géographie régionales. Ottawa: Le Droit, 1938.

Marshall, Herbert. *History of the Ottawa Ski Club*.

Marshall, Herbert. *How Skiing Came to the Gatineau*.

Up the Gatineau! HSG, Old Chelsea, Quebec. Volumes 1 (1975) through 28 (2002).

Up the Gatineau! Gatineau Valley Historical Society, Volume 29, 2003., Old Chelsea, Quebec.

Rezendes, Paul. *Tracking and the Art of Seeing: How to Read Animal Tracks and Sign*. Charlotte, Vermont: Camden House, 1992.

Thomson, Sheila. "Recollections of Early Days in the Gatineau Hills, Collections and Recordings." (Unpublished.)

Von Baeyer, Edwinna. *Garden of Dreams: Kingsmere and Mackenzie King*. Toronto: Dundurn Press, 1990.

Wilson, Alice E. A Guide to the Geology of the Ottawa District. *The Canadian Field Naturalist*, Vol. 70, No. 1, January-March, 1956.

◙ Endnotes

Note: HSG is the Historical Society of the Gatineau (as of 2003, the Gatineau Valley Historical Society); n.d. means no date, n.p. means no publisher.

1. Champlain, Samuel de. *The Voyages and Explorations of Samuel de Champlain (1604-1616) Narrated by Himself, Volume II*; translated by Annie Nettleton Bourne. Toronto: Courier Press 1911, p. 11.

2. Clermont, Norman. "The Archaic Occupation of the Ottawa Valley," in Ottawa Valley Prehistory. Société d'histoire de l'Outaouis, Gatineau, Québec, 1999, pp. 46–49.

3. Champlain. *Journal*. Vol. II, p. 12.

4. Creelman, June. "A Short History of Gatineau Park." NCC, 1978, p. 2.

5. Gillis, Sandra. "The Square Timber Trade in the Ottawa Valley 1806-54." *NCC Interpreter's Manual, Wakefield Mill*. Marcel Lauzière, Gatineau Park, 1985, p. 18.

6. Ibid., p. 22.

7. MacTaggart, John. "Three Years in Canada — An Account of the Actual State of the Country in 1826-7-8." as in *Up the Gatineau!* Vol. 3, HSG, 1977, p. 7.

8. Gard, Anson A. *Genealogy of the Valley: South Hull and Aylmer Edition*. Ottawa: The Emerson Press, 1906, p. 38.

9. Parson, Helen E. "Land Use History of the Gatineau Valley 1800-1850." *Up the Gatineau!* Vol. 9, HSG, 1983, pp. 7–8.

10. Thomson, Sheila. *Recollections of Early Days in the Gatineau Hills, Collections and Recordings*. (Unpublished) p. 96.

11. Ibid., p. 72.

12. Meech, Marion. "Asa Meech." *Up the Gatineau!* Vol. 7, HSG, 1981, p. 15.

13. Ibid., p.15

14. Elliott, Bruce. "The Pink and Moffatt Families of Hull, 1822-38." *Up the Gatineau!* Vol. 1, HSG, 1975, p. 7.

15. Ibid., p. 8.

16. Lafleur, François. "Notes historiques sur le lac Meach." *Seraphicum Bonnes Vacances*, Vol. 1, No. 4, Juillet 1945, Ottawa, p. 13.

17. "Gatineau Park residents find prime ministers make bad neighbors," The *Gazette*, Montreal, 3 May, 1988, p. B1.

18. Bourinot, Arthur S. "Memories of Kingsmere." *The Ottawa Journal*, 25 October, 1963.

19. Gard, Anson A. *Genealogy of the Valley*, p. 47.

20. Ibid., p. 47.

21. Hope, Ethel Penman. "Early Settlement of Meech Lake," n.d. [circa 1925], Unpublished typed speech for Women's Historical Society, NCC historical file H14-701, p. 7.

22. Ibid., p. 8.

23. Gard, Anson A. *Humors of the Valley: South Hull and Aylmer Edition*, Ottawa: Emerson Press, 1906, p. 36.

24. Marshall, Herbert. *History of the Ottawa Ski Club*, n.d., n.p., p.17.

25. Fairbairn, William. "Letter to His Excellency, Sir John Colborn, May 2nd, 1838." Bibliothèque des Archives, Province de Québec.

26. Elman, Eve Lynne. "Wakefield Mill: Mill Owners, the Mill and the Community, 1831-1980." July, 1984, p. 4.

27. Robb, A.B. *History of Wakefield Village*. Wakefield Women's Institute, 1959, p. 10.

28. Geggie, Norma and Stuart. *Lapêche: a History of the Townships of Wakefield and Masham in the Province of Quebec 1792 to 1925*. Old Chelsea, Quebec: HSG, 1980, p. 56b.

29. *Daily Citizen*, June 28, 1877.

30. Newton, Michael. *The Wakefield Gristmill, 1838-1962*, NCC, 1979, p. 58.

31. Hogarth, Donald *Pioneer Mines of the Gatineau Region, Quebec*, University of Ottawa, n.d., p. 13.

32. Ibid., p. 15.

33. Ibid., p. 20.

34. Roberts, Marion. "Carbide Willson: 1860-1915," *Up the Gatineau!* Vol. 2, HSG, 1976, p. 17 ff.

35. Union Carbide promotional booklet, p. 20. NCC Willson historical file.

36. Roberts. p. 22.

37. Ibid., pp. 21–22.

38. Gard, Anson A. *Genealogy of the Valley: South Hull and Aylmer Edition*. Ottawa: Emerson Press, 1906, p. 26.

39. Levy, Gary. "The Ottawa and Gatineau Valley Railway 1871-1901." *Up the Gatineau!*, Vol. 6, HSG, 1990, p. 6.

40. Walton, Lillian. "The Cars of Yesteryear." *Up the Gatineau!* Vol. 12, HSG, 1986, p. 19.

41. Alexis, T.R.P. *Le Canada héroïque et pittoresque*, livre III. Désclée de Brouwer et Cie, Bruges-Paris, 1927, p. 222.

42. Lafleur, François. "Notes historiques sur le lac Meach." *Seraphicum Bonnes Vacances*, Vol. 1, No. 4, Juillet 1945, Ottawa, p. 13.

43. Ibid., p. 15.

44. NCC historical file, #05-0081000-00164.

45. Bourinot, Arthur S. *Some Personal Recollections and Historic Facts about Kingsmere*. Paper read October 8, 1963 to the HSG. Ottawa 1963, pp.4–5.

46. Thomson, Sheila. "Recollections of Early Days in the Gatineau Hills," Collections and Recordings. (unpublished) p. 10.

47. Bourinot, Arthur S. "The Hermit," in *The Collected Poems of Arthur S. Bourinot*.1947.

48. Bourinot. "Some Personal Recollections and Historic Facts About Kingsmere." Paper read October 8, 1963 to the HSG, Ottawa, 1963, 1963, p. 5.

49. Ibid., p. 7.

50. Smythe, Robert. "Mackenzie King's Path to the Waterfall," NCC Interpretation Paper, Ottawa, 1983.

51. Ibid., King's diary entry of September 28, 1927.

52. Ibid., King's diary entry of May 16, 1926.

53. Ibid., King's diary entry of August 11, 1924.

54. King, W.L. Mackenzie. "Last will and testament," Gowling, MacTavish, Watt, Osborne & Henderson, Ottawa, 1950, Will article numbers 22 and 23.

55. Alexis, T. R. P.. *Le Canada héroïque et pittoresque*, livre III. p. 224.

56. Strang, Sheila. "The Alexander Story." *Up the Gatineau!*, Vol. 10, HSG, Old Chelsea, Quebec, 1984, p. 5.

57. Marshall, Herbert. *History of the Ottawa Ski Club*, p. 5.

58. Ibid., p. 10.

59. Ibid., p. 21.

60. Ibid., p. 34.

61. King, W. L. Mackenzie. "Last will and testament," Gowling, MacTavish, Watt, Osborne & Henderson, Ottawa, 1950. (NCC historical files). Will article number 24.

62. NCC. *A Capital in the Making*, NCC, Ottawa, 1998, p. 2.

63. Department of the Interior. "Lower Gatineau Woodlands Survey, Interim Report," Ottawa, 1935, p. 7.

64. Ibid., p. 8.

65. Ibid., pp. 9–10.

66. Ibid., p. 14.

67. Minutes of Proceedings and Evidence, *Joint Committee of the Senate and the House of Commons on the Federal District Commission*, Ottawa 1956, p. 333.

68. Ibid., p. 44.

69. NCC memo dated June 25, 1969, in Meech NCC Historical File #05-0081000-00160.

70. *The Ottawa Citizen*, Friday January 12, 1973. NCC historical file #05-0081000-00160.

71. Marshall, Herbert. *The History of the Ottawa Ski Club*, p. 39.

72. Bowman, Charles A. *Ottawa Editor, The Memoirs of Charles A. Bowman*. Gray's Publishing Ltd., Sidney, B.C. pp. 79–80.

73. Bourinot, Arthur S. "Some Personal Recollections and Historic Facts About Kingsmere," p. 6.

74. Marshall, Herbert. *The History of the Ottawa Ski Club*, pp. 25–26.

75. Thomson, Sheila. "Recollections of Early Days in the Gatineau Hills," p. 99.

76. Ibid., p. 179.

77. Ibid., p. 136.

78. Ibid., pp. 160–161.

◈ About Katharine Fletcher

Katharine Fletcher
Photo credit: The Ottawa Citizen, 88-4715

Katharine is a keen outdoorswoman, author, and freelance writer. She lives with her husband and business partner Eric Fletcher (who created the maps for *Historical Walks*), two horses, and two cats on a heritage farm north of Quyon, Quebec. From this "electronic cottage" Katharine telecommutes with editors and publishers all over the world.

Katharine comes to her love of nature and history naturally. She has fond recollections of childhood rambles at Alderley Edge, England, where, thanks to her mother, she spent happy times walking the wooded ridge overlooking the Cheshire Plain with her family. Ridges and vistas must be in her destiny: "the Edge" is now echoed here at her home beside Gatineau Park, where hikes on the Eardley Escarpment afford breathtaking views of the Ottawa Valley.

Since the first publication of *Historical Walks* (self-published in 1988), Katharine's keen interest in local and natural history has blossomed into an active freelance writing and editing career. Her articles have appeared in a variety of international magazines and newspapers. Since 1989 Katharine has written the Environment Forum for *The Equity*, published in Shawville, Quebec. On May 9, 2003, the Quebec Community Newspaper Association awarded her a certificate of excellence for her work as environmental correspondent. She writes travel columns for *Forever Young*, *Capital Parent* and *Ottawa Life Magazine*, is a frequent contributor to *Ottawa City*, and articles of hers have been published in *The Ottawa Citizen*, *Dallas Morning News*, *Canadian Living*, *Distinction: Elegant Living on Long Island*, *Yankee*, *Moscow Today and Tomorrow*, and many other publications.

Katharine frequently gives seminars on publishing. She also is in demand as interpreter and guide for customized walks, slide shows, and bus tours of the National Capital Region. She is a founder (1989) of the award-winning Pontiac Artists' Studio Tour, was program coordinator for the Ottawa Valley Book Festival (1995), and is a member of the Society of American Travel Writers, Travel Media Association of Canada, Gatineau Valley Historical Society (formerly the Historical Society of the Gatineau), Heritage Ottawa, and is a Friend of the Ottawa Archives.

Katharine has also written *Capital Walks: Walking Tours of Ottawa* and *Capital Rambles: Exploring the National Capital Region*. Both are published by Fitzhenry & Whiteside. She has co-authored a popular guidebook to Quebec with her husband Eric Fletcher: in 2004 the third edition of *Quebec Off the Beaten Path* (Globe Pequot Press) will be published. In addition, Katharine has contributed to four anthologies: *The Canadian Writer's Guide* (12th and 13th Editions, Fitzhenry & Whiteside), *Michelin Green Guide Canada* (Ottawa section, 2001 edition), *Michelin Green Guide Quebec* (Gatineau and Gatineau Park section, 2001 edition), and *Back Roads and Country Getaway Places in Canada* (Reader's Digest Canada, 1997). The second edition of *Historical Walks* was translated into French in 1998, as *Promenades historiques dans la parc de la Gatineau* (Chesley House Publications).

In November 2003, Katharine was thrilled to receive the Ottawa Tourism Media Award, in recognition of her writing, which promotes Ottawa and the National Capital Region as a tourism destination. Previously, she was nominated for a National Newspaper Award (1997), and won third prize for her essay on riding camels in Rajasthan, India, for *Latitudes* magazine.

Gatineau Park Walk Map

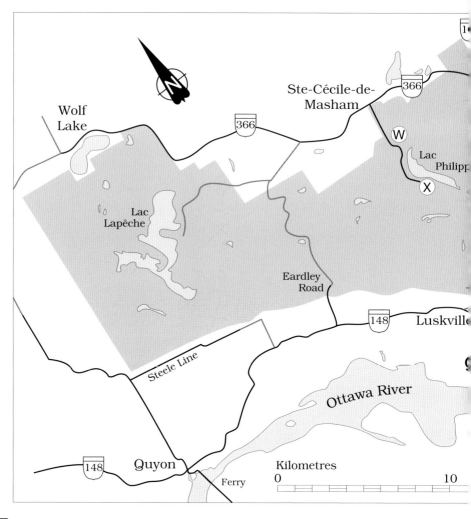

⬚ Key to Walks by Letter and Name

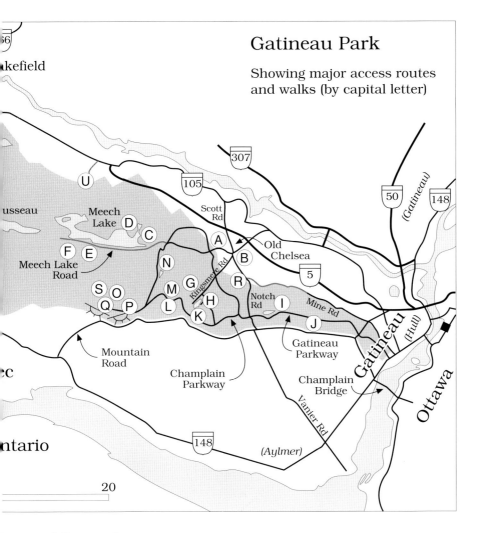

Gatineau Park

Showing major access routes
and walks (by capital letter)

Lakefield

Rousseau

Meech
Lake

Meech Lake
Road

Scott
Rd

Old
Chelsea

Notch
Rd

Mine Rd

Gatineau
Parkway

Mountain
Road

Champlain
Parkway

Champlain
Bridge

Gatineau

Ottawa

(Hull)

(Gatineau)

Vanier Rd

(Aylmer)

Ontario

20

Legend for trail maps

——	Paved road	⌣ Lookout	)(Bridge
——	Unpaved road	⊓ Picnic ground	\ Dam
(P)	Parking	⌂ Lodge	↦ Barrier
🚶	Trailhead	⋁ Lake	✗ Destination marker
- - -	Trail	⌢ Stream	▲ Campground
⋯⋯	Intersecting trail	⫶ Waterfall	105 Highway
(35)	Trail marker	⋇ Swamp	🍁 Trans Canada Trail

◨ Index

Numbers in bold refer to a photograph.